Plots and Plotting

How to create stories that work

Plots and Plotting

How to create stories that work

Diana Kimpton

Kubby Bridge Books

Published by Kubby Bridge Books 2018

©Diana Kimpton 2018

ISBN: 978-1-9998775-0-7

Kubby Bridge Books is an imprint
owned by Diana Kimpton

Contents

Introduction

When I first became an author, I wasn't much good at creating stories. First of all, I tried that technique where you invent some characters and see where they take you. But it failed so badly that my characters wandered off in chapter three, muttering, "Don't think much of this book. It's not going anywhere."

Then I tried writing a list of everything that would happen in each chapter. This was a slight improvement because it helped me complete my first attempt at a children's novel. But that's where the success ended. The story came back from a publisher with a note saying it had "a weak plot and a flat ending".

In retrospect, that was probably a good thing for generations of children because that novel was about an 11-year-old boy who goes to a boarding school for young wizards. This was years before Harry Potter came on the scene so, if my weak plot and flat ending had actually been published, J K Rowling might have been faced with publishers saying, "Tried that, didn't sell."

However, at the time, I could see no advantage in the rejection at all. It shattered my confidence so badly that I went back to producing non-fiction while I tried to learn how to write novels properly. I devoured every book and article I could find about story structure and used my new-found information to analyse the books I read and the movies I watched.

Gradually I started to understand what makes stories work. But I still couldn't write them. That's because story analysis is a different skill from story creation. Analysing a novel or film doesn't reveal anything about how the plot developed in the author's head from the original idea — it only tells you about the finished product.

My personal breakthrough came when I picked up a copy of *How to Write for Animation* by Jeffrey Scott. As I read his step-by-step description of how he used a step outline to develop the story for an episode of *Teenage Mutant Ninja Turtles,* something clicked inside my head. For the first time, I realized that I didn't have to work out a story from beginning to end. I could start at the end and work backwards or start in the middle and work in both directions. Armed with the power of the step outline and the freedom it gave me to work in any way I wanted, I discovered that I could finally create stories that worked.

Since then, I've written twenty-three novels for young people, including my Pony-Mad Princess series which has sold a million copies worldwide. I've come a long way since that devastating rejection, and I hope this book will help you make similar progress whether you write for adults or for children.

Of course, there are probably as many ways of writing stories as there are authors in the world. We all think differently and work differently. So this book isn't about getting you to create stories my way. It's about giving you the understanding and the tools you need to discover how to create stories your way.

To help make my ideas clearer, I'll be using some of my own books as examples as well as developing a plot especially for this book. The reason for concentrating on my own work isn't to show off. It's because these are the only stories where I know for sure how they were created. However much we analyse other people's stories, we can never be sure of how they grew in their authors' minds.

1

To plot or not to plot

Raising the issue of plotting with any random group of authors is likely to start a heated discussion. Some think plotting destroys creativity. Others believe that creativity flounders without plot. Personally, I think the argument is pointless because creativity, story and plot are so intrinsically bound together that it's not possible to separate them.

When we set out to create a story, we are starting on a journey of discovery and, as with most journeys, there are alternative routes we can take that all end up in the same place. Which one we choose depends on what works best for us personally, and it may not be the same for each story. For example, I wrote the first draft of my funny sci-fi story, *Alien Sheep*, with only a rough idea of where the story was going, and then added an extra strand to the story during some fairly major rewrites. In contrast, I plotted *Princess Ellie's Summer Holiday* in huge detail before I started writing and hardly rewrote the first draft at all, except to tweak the language.

I suspect that much of the strong anti-plot feeling amongst authors is due to a dislike of the formulaic plotting methods and strict story structure taught in some creative writing classes. It may also be due to differences in our understanding of what plot and plotting actually are.

For me, the plot is the plan of the story and plotting is the creation of that plan, whether we do it in our heads or write it down.

So maybe planning is a less contentious word than plotting. Unless we truly believe that monkeys pressing keys at random might eventually produce the works of Shakespeare, we all plan to some extent before we start writing, so if you really have trouble with me talking about plotting, please think about planning instead.

2

When's the right time to write

The less planning you do before you start writing, the higher the chance that you'll have to do extensive rethinking and rewriting after you've completed your first draft. That's why I think the *start writing and see where your characters go* approach should be called *write first, plot later*. It failed me completely, but I know other writers like to work that way so I'm not going to tell you not to try it. However, if you're the sort of writer who hates making major changes to stories after you've finished them, you'll get a better result by working out the details of your story before you start writing.

It's fair to point out that having a complete plot worked out doesn't rule out a later flash of inspiration that calls for big changes, and it definitely doesn't mean that you should ignore that additional inspiration if it comes. The plotting process is there to help you channel your creativity – not restrict it.

It's entirely up to you when you switch from plotting to writing, and you can switch back again any time you like. For example, I often write a scene or two quite early on so I can try out different viewpoints (more on that later) before I go back to the plotting process. This kind of test scene can also be useful when you're developing characters. Writing scraps of dialogue can help you work out their individual voices and see how they relate to each other. If nothing else, it may make you realize they are too similar and send you back to your mental drawing board.

A good compromise between the two extremes of plot first or plot later is to work out the shape of the entire story but leave the details until you actually start the writing. So you plot the opening in detail and write that. Then work out the details of the next few scenes and write them. And so on. This approach is *plot, write, plot, write, plot, write, etc.* And you don't have to do it in sequence. Some writers like to concentrate on planning and writing the most important scenes in their book before they work out how the scenes link together.

Experiment a bit to discover which approach works best for you, and don't be surprised if, like me, you find that your approach varies with each book. This is because different ideas develop differently in our heads. If the inspiration for your story is a final scene that fell fully formed into your head, you may want to write that down before you decide what came before it.

3

The basic components of a good story

We meet stories all the time – by listening, by reading and by watching on screen – so you and I have been absorbing the basics of storytelling all our lives without realizing it. That probably explains why, in the early days of my career, I occasionally managed to write a good story without understanding how I did it. That success came more by luck and intuition than by skill, and it only worked for short stories. As soon as I tried to write anything longer, I got lost and ended up floundering. Maybe you're in the same situation.

In order to create consistently good stories, you need to understand how they work. Because this is so important, there are plenty of books available that delve deeply into story structure. Some of them are brilliant, but some drown you with jargon and suggest that three act structure or mythic structure or whatever is the current fashion is the only way to tell a story.

Taken to extremes, this can be a disaster. I was once commissioned to turn a Victorian children's book into a feature film. The young and, it turned out, fairly inexperienced producer asked, "You do understand three act structure, don't you?"

"Yes," I replied, suddenly glad that I'd read all those books.

"So you know that the inciting incident has to happen on page 35."

"No, it doesn't," I argued. "It happens when the story needs it."

By the way, if you've never heard of an inciting incident before, Robert McKee defines it in his book, *Story,* as "the first major event of the telling" and "the primary cause for all that follows". But don't worry about that too much. The term is part of the jargon for analysing stories that have already been written. It's not important to the art of creating them, and you'll automatically put an inciting incident in your story, whether you know the term or not.

The key to a story's success is to make the reader or viewer care about what is happening. If they don't care, they'll stop turning the pages, switch to another TV station or concentrate on their popcorn at the cinema. But if you really capture their interest and make them care, they'll lean forward in their seats and concentrate on every word. They'll be so eager to find out what happens next that they won't be able to put your book down and, in the case of children, they'll continue reading long after they should have been asleep.

To be this successful, your story needs to have several components.

- One or more main characters your readers can relate to strongly enough to care what happens to them. (In story structure jargon, they are the protagonists.)

- A problem that the main character has to solve and which the readers can understand and care about.

- A sequence of events where the main character struggles to solve the problem, meeting difficulties along the way.

- A final difficulty that seems so insurmountable that all appears lost. This is sometimes called the black moment, and it's a heart-in-mouth time for the readers.

- The final crisis where the main character has one last try and solves the problem. It's important that they do this by themselves, even if they have help from their companions. Having someone else solve the problem is not satisfying for the readers.

You probably already know that all stories need to have a beginning, a middle and an end. These three parts correspond exactly with the three acts that experts in analysing stories call three act structure. Here's how the components listed above fit into those three sections.

- **The beginning** or **act one** – sets up the main character and the problem.

- **The middle** or **act two** – moves on to the attempts to solve the problem, up to and including the black moment.

- **The end** or **act three** – contains the climax and the final success.

Of course, the characters in most stories are human, but they don't have to be. The same skills you use when writing about people can make your readers care about any character who has emotions, including animals, aliens, toys and robots. Books for young children frequently feature this type of character, but older readers can enjoy looking at the world through non-human eyes too. In fact, the different perspective this provides can be useful if you want your story to provide insights into human behaviour.

4

How theory works in practice

To see a good story in action, let's take a look at my first and most successful picture book, *The Bear Santa Claus Forgot*. It's delighted thousands of children and was one of the Children's Book Council Choices for 1996 so I know the story works. It also illustrates all the characteristics of a good story in just over 800 words.

I've put the text of the story in a different font to help you separate it from my comments.

* * * * *

Christmas Eve was nearly over. Santa Claus yawned. Just one more visit to make and then he could go home.

This sets the time and place and provides a reason why Santa might be forgetful. Notice that I don't go into whether his tiredness is caused by a surfeit of mince pies and sherry because that's not relevant to this story.

The sleigh landed gently on Madeleine's roof. Santa Claus put the last few toys into a sack and swung it onto his back. But the sack was old. It had a hole in one corner.

At this point, the picture shows a teddy bear's leg sticking out through the hole.

> *"Eeek," said the bear, as he slid through the hole.*

Here's our main character.

> *"Ouch," said the bear, as he landed with a bump on the floor of the sleigh.*
>
> *He sat up and rubbed his head. He could see Santa climbing down Madeleine's chimney without him. That wasn't right.*
>
> *He was Madeleine's bear. The label round his neck said so. She had asked Santa for him weeks ago. What would she say in the morning when he wasn't there?*

Here's our main character's problem – he's not been delivered. And there's something important at stake – Madeleine's happiness. We don't want her to be sad so we start to care what happens.

> *When Santa came back, he didn't notice the teddy bear sitting all by himself. He just climbed onto the sleigh and whistled to his reindeer. They galloped away, pulling the sleigh up into the night sky.*

The problem's getting worse. There seems little chance now that Santa will notice the bear in time to deliver him.

> *First the sleigh turned to the right.*
>
> *"Oops," said the bear, as he tumbled across the floor.*
>
> *"Ouch," said the bear, as he bumped into the side of the sleigh.*
>
> *Then the sleigh turned to the left.*
>
> *"Oops," said the bear, as he tumbled across the floor.*

"Ouch," said the bear, as he bumped into the other side of the sleigh.

Next the front of the sleigh pointed up into the air, as the reindeer galloped higher and higher.

"Oops," said the bear, as he tumbled across the floor.

"Help," cried the bear, as he bounced out of the back of the sleigh.

Just as you're lulled by the bear sliding about, an unexpected plot turn brings another problem. Is the bear going to fall?

The bear grabbed desperately for something to save him. As the sleigh flew off, the teddy bear dangled from the back by his front paws.

Hurray. He's saved himself. Clever bear.

"Phew," said the bear, as he held on very tight. His paws ached, but at least he was safe. Then he looked down and saw the roof of Madeleine's house far below him. "That's where I should be," he thought. "If Santa won't take me, I'll have to go by myself."

This is a major turning point in the story. It's where the bear takes matters into his own paws and decides to solve his problem himself. It's also where the beginning turns into the middle.

The bear shut his eyes and let go.

"Aaargh," said the bear, as he fell through the air.

"Eek," said the bear, as he spun round and round with his arms and legs outstretched.

He's doing this for Madeleine even though he's frightened. This helps us see how brave he is and how much he cares about her and this, in turn, helps us care about him.

"Ouch," said the bear, as he landed with a thump on Madeleine's roof.

He sat up and blew some snow off the end of his nose. The snow was cold and damp. It made his hair go spiky.

I wish you could see the picture that goes with this bit. It's my favourite in the whole book.

The bear scrambled up a pile of snow and looked down the chimney.

Inside it was dark and scary. He didn't want to go down there, but how else could he get into Madeleine's house?

Another problem and another test of the bear's resolve. Is he brave enough to go down the chimney for Madeleine?

Oooh," said the bear, as he climbed nervously into the chimney pot.

"Aaargh," cried the bear, as he slid down the chimney.

He's very scared, but he does it anyway which makes us like him more and more.

"Ouch," said the bear, as he landed in the fireplace with a cloud of soot and ash.

There was no Christmas stocking by the fireplace.

There was no Christmas stocking under the tree.

Oh no! We thought he'd solved the problem but he hasn't.

"It must be beside Madeleine's bed," thought the bear so he started to climb the stairs.

The stairs were very tall for a bear. The stairs were very steep for a bear.

Another problem, but he doesn't give up. This is a very determined bear and we love him for it.

"Phew," said the bear when he got to the top. He wanted to stop for a rest, but he couldn't. He had to hurry. It was nearly morning.

A bit of added time pressure to up the tension. Now he hasn't just got to deliver himself – he's got to do it quickly.

He walked along the landing and peeped around the first door.

"Hmmm," said the bear with a shake of his head. He could hear a dripping tap. He could smell soap.

This wasn't Madeleine's room.

First try doesn't work

He peeped around the second door.

"Hmmm," said the bear with a shake of his head. He could see a big bed with two people in it. He could hear snoring.

This wasn't Madeleine's room.

Second try doesn't work.

He peeped around the third door. "Ah ha," said the bear. He could see a little girl fast asleep. He could see a Christmas stocking hanging on the end of her bed.

This must be Madeleine's room.

Third try succeeds. For a brief moment, it looks as if he's won.

But the stocking was very high for a bear.

"Oh," said the bear, with a tear in his eye. There was no way he could get into Madeleine's stocking. There was no way he could be a proper Christmas present, unless...

This is the black moment. All seems lost because he's too small to complete the task. And now the middle of the story moves on to the end.

"Hmm," said the bear, as he scratched his head thoughtfully. In the corner of the room were some leftover Christmas decorations.

"Ho ho," said the bear, as he rolled himself up in a sheet of wrapping paper.

Clever bear has come up with another solution.

"Eeek," said the bear, as he fell flat on his back.

"Aah," said the bear, as he looked up at the stocking.

He was badly wrapped up, a little bit damp and rather sooty, but he was in just the right place – well, nearly, anyway.

Success at last – well nearly, anyway.

That's where Madeleine found him in the morning, and she loved him straight away.

An ending designed to produce a sigh of satisfaction. It's just what we wanted to happen, and the bear has achieved it entirely by his own efforts.

* * * *

You'll notice that I've described how this story works without using any of the jargon often used in story structure books and courses.

That's partly because I didn't want to introduce terms that you don't need to know, but also because the story itself is more important than the words we use to analyse it.

Too much reliance on jargon can cause confusion. In this story, some people might say that the inciting incident in this story is when the bear falls out of the sack. Some might be sure it's when Santa goes down Madeleine's chimney without him, and others might think it's when he falls out of the sleigh. That's because story analysis is not an exact science.

It's hard enough to agree which is the inciting incident in this straightforward short story, but, once you're looking at a full-length novel or script with multiple storylines, the situation becomes really confused. So my advice is not to worry. Leave the story analysis to the experts after you've finished your book. You can write stories that work without knowing all the jargon.

5

The magic of three

I don't know why, but there's something about the number three that resonates with our souls and gives us satisfaction. That's why it is woven through the fabric of storytelling through the ages. Stories have three parts and trilogies have three books. Shakespeare had three witches, the wolf tried to catch the three little pigs and Goldilocks stole the porridge from the three bears. More recently, Harry Potter, Hermione and Ron faced danger together, hindered by Draco Malfoy, Crabbe and Goyle.

The magic of three doesn't just apply to the number of characters in stories. It works with events as well, which is why so many movies make the struggling hero try once and fail, try a second time and fail and finally succeed on the third attempt.

Three repeats even works at the level of the words we choose to use. "I'll huff and I'll blow your house down" or "I'll puff and I'll blow your house down" don't have the same rhythm and completeness as "I'll huff and I'll puff and I'll blow your house down". Similarly the big wolf, the bad wolf and even the big, bad, brown wolf don't roll off our tongues as easily as the big, bad wolf.

When we were analysing *The Bear Santa Claus Forgot*, I pointed out that he tries twice to find Madeleine's room without success and then succeeds on the third attempt. But the number crops up in other places in the story too. For example, the sleigh turns to the right, then to the left and then up into the air while the bear slides one way, then the other and then falls out of the back. He sometimes speaks in groups of three as well.

"Oooh," said the bear, as he climbed nervously into the chimney pot.

"Aaargh," cried the bear, as he slid down the chimney.

"Ouch," said the bear, as he landed in the fireplace with a cloud of soot and ash.

However, he doesn't always do that. The magic of three can become boring if you use it too much and always grouping events in threes can make your story too predictable. So keep that magic number in mind and use it whenever it helps the story work, but don't feel you have to use it all the time.

6

Finding ideas

The Ancient Greeks believed in the Muses: supernatural beings who send ideas to creative people. The late, great Terry Pratchett talked about ideas floating around in the atmosphere, ready to pop into our brains at random. Both theories suggest that ideas come from somewhere outside us, and maybe some of them do.

The story that you read earlier was inspired by a picture that came into my head of Santa's sleigh flying through the air with a teddy bear hanging from the back by his front paws. That picture arrived unannounced and unbidden – I wasn't even thinking about writing a story at the time. I don't know if the idea floated into my head or it was sent by the Muses or came from somewhere else, but I may not have been the only person who received it. While my story was being illustrated, another picture book was published with a front cover that showed a bear hanging by his front paws from the back of Santa's sleigh. The other author's story was different from mine, but I strongly suspect that same inspirational picture had popped into both our heads.

Unexpected ideas don't always come from nowhere like the forgotten bear. Sometimes they are triggered by a chance encounter, an item in a newspaper or something someone says. But they always arrive without warning which is why the standard advice for all writers is to carry a notebook at all times.

I'm passing on that advice because it sounds like a sensible thing to do, although I have to admit that I don't do it myself. Which explains why I can't remember the best idea I ever had. I can only remember that I had it and, as I was in the shower at the time, a notebook wouldn't have helped anyway. Neither would the modern alternative: a mobile phone. I know one author who texts herself her ideas instead of writing them down on paper.

Unfortunately, unexpected ideas are just that – unexpected. We can't rely on them turning up when we need them. Which is a pain because, as writers, we need ideas all the time – an initial one to get a project started and dozens of others to help us develop it into a full-length novel or script. So when the Muses have deserted us and none of the floating ideas are coming our way, we need to do some work to make inspiration happen.

Brainstorming and Mind Maps

One way to get your creative juices flowing is to brainstorm. This involves focusing on one particular issue or question and writing down as many ideas as you can think of. Let your imagination run riot and, if it helps, seek inspiration by delving into your memory of things that have happened to you or other people.

You are aiming for quantity rather than quality, so don't make any attempt to judge the ideas at this stage. Just write down everything that comes into your head, including thoughts you think are too silly to bother with. You may discover later that they contain the germ of an idea that you can use. I find it helpful to brainstorm for a set period of time, because forcing myself to keep going after I've thought of all the obvious ideas often results in real originality.

To demonstrate how brainstorming works, I'll show you how I came up with the initial idea for *There Must Be Horses*. I knew I wanted to write a horse book for readers of 10+ with a girl as the main character and the emphasis on horse care rather than winning trophies. So I brainstormed all the possibilities and ended up with a list like this:

- Girl lives at country hotel where guests can bring their own horses and have a riding holiday. Way out in country, like another world.

- Isolated place. I loved stories set in the Australian outback when I was young. Aim for a similar feel but not Aussie.

- Brat camp. Kids with problems come to somewhere and are healed by ponies.

- Maybe just setting up riding holidays at a farm – cleaning out stables, etc.

- Something happened to Dad. Don't know what. Accident rather than illness or maybe lost job. Farming in a downturn.

- Is the hotel/farm family home? Been in family for generations – was Grandad's. Did family lose their home in a financial crash?

- Has girl got a pony? Maybe he's old/useless/scruffy/ wild pony off the moor.

- Does Mum ride? Is Jenny the only pony-mad one in family/village?

- Mum and Dad are both writers and leave Jenny to her own devices. Country cottage is rented. Can't pay rent. Face eviction.

- Jenny lost pony. Doesn't want to ride any more . Friend will lend her hers, but she won't use it. Losing her pony was too painful. Then parents suggest running riding holidays. She's resistant, but it's the only way to save the hotel.

- Make the place remote. Far from towns. Small village some distance away. Schooling difficult.

- If Dad is a writer, maybe they moved here because the isolation helps his creativity.

- Livery stables. Family have land, house, stable yard, milking cows, etc.

- Sasha keeps her pony at the stables at the big house.

- Sasha lives on a farm.

- In future, cars are banned. Have to use horses.

- Live action role-playing. People come to farm to pretend to live in the past.

- Sasha in care. Sent to first-time foster carers who run a stables/rescue home/do riding lessons. She wants to stay but it's only a temporary placement. Can she persuade them to keep her?

As you can see, that's a list of random notes – not titles. (Those come later, often when the book is finished.) Some of the ideas overlap, some don't mention horses and some were completely unexpected – I really wasn't aiming at science fiction. I dwelt a lot on setting because I knew it was going to affect possible storylines, and I experimented a bit with the girl's name. Most importantly, the idea that eventually formed the basis for the book was the last one, which shows the importance of not giving up too soon.

I wrote those ideas in a list, but it's often easier to link them together if you draw a Mind Map (or spider graph) instead. That involves putting the thing you are focusing on in the middle of a large sheet of paper and drawing arrows out from it in all directions that lead to your ideas. From those ideas, you draw more arrows leading to further possibilities, and you can also draw other arrows linking the various possibilities together.

I love Mind Maps because of the way they help you investigate the way ideas connect so I use them a lot at all stages of plotting. Here's one showing some ideas for a story about an animal thief.

If you want to keep your ideas even more fluid, you can put each thought on a sticky note and lay them out on a table in whatever pattern appeals to you. This makes it easy to move things about, and you can use your phone to photograph the final result to help you remember everything.

Analysing the results

When you've finished brainstorming, give yourself a break to clear your mind. Then look at what you've written with a fresh eye. Do any of your ideas stand out from the others? Do any of them fill you with excitement? If so, you've found your project.

If you've got two or more possible choices that look equally good, try playing with them a little to discover which has the most potential or try combining them to make another idea that's even better. And if none of your ideas appeal, pick a different starting point and try brainstorming again. Don't despair and don't rush. You're going to be working on this story for a long time so take your time and find an idea you really like.

Using real events

Sometimes your idea for a novel may be triggered by something from the past: an historical event, your own life story, your great-grandfather's diary or a set of love letters discovered in a junk shop. This type of information can provide an excellent starting point for a story, but you'll need to be careful not to let it become a straightjacket that restricts your plot.

Although truth is sometimes stranger than fiction, it can also be rambling, repetitious or just plain boring. And telling your readers "That's what really happened" won't keep them reading once they have lost interest. So always remember that you are writing fiction, not a history textbook. That means you don't have to include everything that happened in real life. You can also add extra events and characters, invent details and generally do everything you need to make the story work and hold your readers' attention.

7

A note about themes

The theme of a book is the underlying message that it carries. Many successful novels have strong themes like love, forgiveness or belonging that help readers relate to the characters and care about what happens next. However, concentrating too much on theme during the creation process can get you into trouble and result in a story that's so contrived and unbelievable that no one wants to read it. This is particularly likely if your main reason for writing a book for children is to give your readers a strong moral message.

This doesn't mean that it's wrong to start off with a desire to show that bullying is wrong or drugs ruin lives. It just means that you mustn't let that theme dominate your plotting process. Instead, start by creating characters or events that will bring your issue to life. Then put your message to one side and concentrate on creating a strong story about people (or animals) that your readers will care about.

In my experience, the theme of a book usually looks after itself so I don't worry about it very much. Even when I don't have one in mind when I start plotting a new book, a theme often appears without me consciously thinking about it. It's revealed by the events of the story and, once I've realized it's there, I can go back through my plot or first draft, tweaking events slightly to make it stronger.

Whether your theme comes first or you find it later, there is no need to tell the readers what it is. Give them the pleasure of discovering it for themselves. If the only way to get over the moral of your book is to write it down on the last page, you haven't told the story well enough.

8

Starting to develop your story

Once you have your basic idea, you are ready to start developing it further. This is the point at which those people who feel strongly about the "To plot or not to plot" question start asking if your book is going to be character-led or plot-driven. In my opinion, the question doesn't make sense because the events of the story affect the characters and the characters affect the events. So the plot and the characters are so closely intertwined that it's impossible to tease them apart.

The division of books into character-led or plot-driven is something that comes after they are written. It keeps reviewers happy and gives something for story analysts to do but, just like the inciting incident, it's not important to the creative process. What is important is that, before you can start plotting in detail, you have an idea of the main character(s), the problem they face and the setting of the story. You don't have to decide on them in that order, but you do need all three.

Why you always need characters

If your idea is predominantly about an earthquake, a war or some other major event, it's tempting to think that characters aren't important. But without them, your novel would be more like a documentary than a story – a factual account of what happens without the tension and excitement that holds readers' attention. To capture their interest and make them care about what happens, you need to make those events personal by showing how the characters involved in the situation are affected.

That's why war films focus closely on individual soldiers, and disaster movies focus on the people whose lives are in danger and/or those who are trying to save them. It's also the reason why directors often add a small child or a dog to tug at the audience's heartstrings, but that isn't compulsory and it can look hackneyed if you're not careful. (Similar hackneyed ideas explain why I'm always wary of travelling by plane if there's a nun on board.)

What defines characters?

Let's imagine a tall, slim girl with long, blonde hair and blue eyes. We'll call her Jane. Do you feel sympathy for her? No. Do you care what happens to her? No. That's because the facts I've given you so far only tell you what she looks like. They don't tell you anything about what she's like as a person. It's not appearance that determines who someone is – it's how they react to people and situations and the reasons they react that way.

What type of person we want Jane to be depends on the part we want her to play in our story and what that story is about. But our decisions about her will also affect how the story develops. Let's imagine we're working on a science fiction book about an alien invasion and think through some possibilities.

Jane looks like a stereotypical dumb blonde so the easy option is to cast her as a passive victim, screaming in terror while she waits to be rescued from evil extraterrestrials. However, easy options produce predictable plots and they, in turn, produce bored readers. That's why I'm going to turn the stereotype on its head and make Jane clever at something. Exactly what that should be depends on what she needs to do in the story. So let's play with some possible skills she could have and see where they might lead.

Skill 1: Businesswoman

Jane has a flair for buying and selling – a talent that's already made her a fortune. But, for reasons we haven't decided yet, she is not satisfied. She always wants more. When the aliens arrive, she sees them as a vast untapped market. No longer content to sell only to her own world, she tries to join with the invaders so she can market to the universe. This brings her into conflict with the other citizens of the town who see her actions as betrayal.

Skill 2: Doctor

Jane has dedicated her life to helping sick children and preserving life. When the invaders arrive, she joins up with a small group of medics willing to fight to protect their patients. Then an injured alien comes to her for help. Should she let him die or does the Hippocratic Oath apply to all life, not just humans?

Skill 3: Linguist

Shy and reserved, Jane spends her days deep in the basement of the university, deciphering texts written in long-lost languages. When she translates some alien messages, she realizes there is a way to make peace with the new arrivals. Can she stop the government from killing the aliens unnecessarily and sparking a war across the universe?

These three different skills produce three very different Janes with three different problems which, in turn, give us three very different stories. She looks the same in all three so it's not Jane's appearance that's affecting the story – it's the way she responds to the challenges she faces. So when you think up characters, concentrate on who they are rather than what they look like.

Setting

You don't have to know much detail about the setting yet, but it helps to have a rough idea of where and when your story is going to take place as that will affect what happens. A murder mystery set in a closed community of nuns will be quite different from one set in the middle of a busy city; and a romance set in an Elizabethan palace will be very different from one in a hippy community in the 1970s. Once again, keep details to a minimum at this stage. If your story doesn't demand a specific setting – 18th century Paris or the battlefields of the American Civil War – you can get away with just a vague idea of period and place at this stage and add the details later.

Why there must be a problem

A man on a boat is just a character in a setting. To turn it into a story, you need to give him a problem. If we make the boat very small, put it in the middle of an ocean and add a fierce tiger as the only other passenger, the man faces a life-or-death struggle to survive and we've got a story. But don't rush off and write it. Yann Martel got there first with *The Life of Pi*.

Not all stories need a tiger, but you definitely need to give your main character a problem. That needs to be something your readers will relate to, although it doesn't have to be a problem they will have actually experienced. That's particularly important to remember when you're writing for children. Even pre-schoolers understand about love, loneliness, fear and taking risks so they can enjoy a wider range of stories than many people realize.

What next?

Once you have at least one character, a problem and a setting, you have the basic ingredients for your story. But before you start plotting in more detail, there is one more thing to think about and you can find out more about that in the next section.

9

It's never too soon to think of the ending

Your plot is the route for your writing journey. When you are travelling by car, it's impossible to decide which roads to take until you know where you are going and, in the same way, it's easier to plot a book or movie if you decide early on what the end will be. Once you have that, you'll find there are many possible paths you can take to reach your final destination and part of the plotting process is deciding which of these you will use. Maybe that's why plotting often makes me feel like a detective discovering a story that wants to be told.

This doesn't mean that you need to know the ending in huge detail before you start. A vague idea of what's going to happen is quite good enough and leaves room for surprising twists and turns along the way. Will the romantic couple decide to stay together forever? Will the detective find the murderer, or will the hero succeed in saving everyone from the volcano? Once you know that, you can work backwards from the ending to see what needs to happen earlier in the story to enable that ending to take place and, as you decide those points, you'll find that you can plot the end in more detail.

For example, your detective can't solve the murder until one's been committed so you need to decide who's been murdered, where the body was found and how your detective becomes involved with the case. You also need to decide who the murderer is and why they killed the victim so you can work out the clues that will help your detective solve the crime. As that all becomes clearer in your head, you'll be able to work out the ending in more detail and decide on the final confrontation with the killer.

What makes a good ending?

The ending of a story has a big effect on the reader and plays a large part in making them decide whether to recommend the book or movie to other people. In order to satisfy the reader, the end needs to bring the storyline to a successful conclusion by showing the main characters solving their main problem in a way that's believable and makes readers feel that natural justice has been done (which isn't always the same as legal justice).

As I mentioned earlier, they also need to solve that problem themselves so it's best to make sure that any necessary help turns up as late as possible. For example, if you need the police there to arrest the villains, try to make them turn up after your hero has overcome the ringleader, defused the bomb or otherwise foiled the evil plan.

Your end doesn't have to be totally happy, but a sad ending can be depressing unless it's handled carefully. It's best to leave your readers with at least some hope at the end, even if they are crying at the same time. This is particularly true if your chosen ending involves the death of one or more of your main characters. Readers will accept this more willingly if the world is a better place for their sacrifice so they didn't die in vain. You can also take away some of the sadness of a character dying by showing that they freely chose to let that happen. In the movie *Gladiator*, our sadness about the death of Maximus is tempered by the fact that he wanted to be reunited with his dead wife and son and by the fact that he gave his life avenging their deaths.

It's also important that your ending is clear and makes sense. If you suddenly introduce magic to a story that hasn't contained any before or you don't say whether the main character survives or not, you'll end up with confused readers who won't recommend your book. You don't have to tie up every loose end, especially if you're planning a sequel, but you do need to bring the story to a satisfactory conclusion and maybe hint at what the future holds.

10

Step outlines – the powerful way to plot

Once you're ready to start plotting, the most powerful tool you can use is a step outline. That's just what the name suggests – an outline of the steps of the story. And the reason it's so useful is that you don't have to develop your plot from the beginning to the end as you would if you used the "start writing and see where your characters take you" technique. Instead, you can start at the end and work backwards or in the middle and work both ways or jump around wherever you like. Better still, you can do all that without losing sight of the overall shape of the story.

Over the years, I've discovered that the best way to explain how to use step outlines is to show you the process in action. But before I start doing that, I need to tell you a bit more about them.

A step outline is not a chapter by chapter outline

Chapters and steps are not the same thing. Steps vary in size enormously, but chapters are usually much the same length. As a result, some chapters may contain several steps while a big step might need to be spread over two chapters with a cliffhanger at the end of the first one. It's hard to tell exactly how big the steps will be until you start writing them so fixing the chapter breaks at the planning stage can act like a straightjacket, preventing you from making the most of dramatic events through lack of space. It will also restrict your ability to deviate from the plan when inspiration strikes.

I suspect that these problems with chapter-by-chapter outlines are what turns people off plotting. But step outlines don't restrict you in the same way – they just keep you working in the right direction while leaving you the flexibility to make your scenes as long or short as you wish. I usually find that chapter breaks occur naturally while I'm doing the actual writing, although I sometimes write large sections as continuous prose and put in the chapter breaks later. This works particularly well with action sequences and the final crisis.

A step outline is not set in stone

If you think of creating a story as a journey of discovery, your step outline is your roadmap. And just as with a real journey, there is nothing to stop you exploring interesting-looking diversions or changing the route to one that looks better.

I find that knowing where I'm going frees up my creativity. I can concentrate on making each individual scene as good as it can be, because I know where it fits in the overall structure of the story. In the process, I often spot a new way to develop the plot or I introduce a minor character who is so good that they need more to do. When that happens, I pause for a while to rejig the step outline so it incorporates the change. Then I go on writing.

When I was working on *Princess Ellie's Perfect Plan*, I plotted the book carefully before I started the actual writing and created a detailed step outline that I thought would work. But halfway through writing the story, I realized I'd made a mistake. The second half had too little action and too much introspection. Worse still for a pony book, it had far too little stuff with ponies.

So I brainstormed ideas, reordered some of the steps in the outline, cut others out completely and introduced a major new problem in the shape of an angry bull. These were huge changes that would have really hurt if I'd already written the whole book, but the step outline helped me make them painlessly and fine-tune the action and tension to give the story exactly the right pace. In fact, when I finally sent the book to my editor, she said it was so good that I should give masterclasses in plotting. She had no idea how near it had come to disaster!

The practicalities of step outlining

In this book, I'm writing each step outline as a numbered list, and that's how I always write the final version I use as a base for my writing. The numbered list facility in the software you use for writing is perfect for this as the numbering will adjust automatically as you add, take away or move steps. You'll also find a step outlining facility built into some specialist writing software. (I used *Snowflake Pro* successfully for *There Must Be Horses.*)

However, during the early stages of the plotting process, I sometimes find that I am more creative if I don't use my computer at all. Instead, I write each step by hand on a sticky notelet. Then I stick those together in a long line that I can easily peel apart to insert a new step wherever it's needed or to move an existing step to another place.

It's hugely satisfying to see your plot grow physically like this, and you can add extra sophistication by using different coloured notelets for different characters or for different strands of your story to help you see how they weave together. Although it becomes a bit unwieldy for long plots, it's a powerful technique that works for writers of all levels of experience. When I've taught it in school workshops, the teachers assured me it was the first time all their children produced stories with a beginning, a middle and an end.

Some people prefer to use postcards instead of sticky notes. Others prefer to write the list by hand on a white board or to use software specially designed for step outlining. The exact technique you choose doesn't matter. Use the power of the step outline in whichever way works best for you.

11

Step outlining in action

The easiest way to explain how step outlining works is to show you the process in action. So, while I'm writing this book, I'm going to plot a brand-new story to let you see how I do it.

Of course, that means I need an idea so I've gone back to the one we thought of earlier where Jane was an expert in deciphering ancient languages. I've added a second character – a geeky guy called Seb – and I've ditched the invading aliens because I don't want to write a war story. But Jane still works in a university or museum (setting), and she still discovers an important secret when she deciphers a mysterious message (problem). I've also decided that the book is set in the future (more setting) and its working title is *Future Proof*. That's probably not what the book will be called if it ever gets published, but it gives me something to call it until then.

Here's my initial very short step outline:

1. Jane translates a message.

2. The message contains a secret that affects the future safety of mankind.

3. Jane alerts important people.

4. Mankind is saved.

That gives us the basic structure of our story. Now it's time to fill out some details and, to do that, I'm going to look at each step and think about what needs to happen before it.

Before Jane can translate the message, she has to find it or be given it. If she gets it as part of her job, she'd just tell her superior what she's found and that would be the end of the story. So she needs to get it some other way – maybe one that means the existence of the message itself has to be secret. Enter Seb – the geeky guy. Let's make him give her the message.

But why does it have to stay secret? Time for a bit of brainstorming that helps me decide that this future world is authoritarian. Knowledge is strictly controlled, and independent historical research is banned. Having discovered the message hidden in an ancient artefact (not sure what yet), Seb is unwilling to hand it to his bosses without discovering what it says. So the step outline becomes:

1. Seb accidentally drops an exhibit in the museum while he is cleaning it. It opens and he finds a message inside. But it's not in English.

2. Seb starts to take it to his boss but hesitates. He looks at the message again. Someone's gone to the trouble of hiding it. Maybe it's important to keep it secret.

3. He takes it to Jane and asks her to translate it.

4. Jane won't do it. There's a law against independent research and she doesn't want to get into trouble.

5. Seb persuades her to change her mind. (Don't know how yet.)

6. Jane discovers that the message contains information that affects the future safety of mankind.

7. Jane alerts important people.

8. Mankind is saved.

As you can see, I'm adding problems and dilemmas for our two characters as I add steps. Will Seb hand in the message? Will Jane be willing to take the risk of translating it? As the characters struggle with those questions and make their decisions, they start to grow in my mind and become more real.

You'll notice that step 5 is rather vague. That's because I've currently no idea why Jane should change her mind. But I've put the step in anyway to show that it's needed, and I'll work out the details later, once I know more about Jane. I often put in vague steps like that when I'm step outlining – even putting "stuff happens" reminds me that there's a space in the story that needs to be filled.

Step 6 is vague too and I can't go much further without deciding some more details about the message. So it's back to brainstorming and Mind Maps for a while, before I decide that the information it contains reveals how the ruthless elite who rule the world can be defeated.

Wow! Sudden inspiration. Suppose it's not a written message at all. Suppose it's an extremely old mobile phone that's still working. Seb doesn't understand technology, but he knows Jane does. She's in charge of the security at the museum and runs all the alarm systems. That would avoid the need for the message to be in a language Seb can't understand, and it also gives Jane a skill that may be much more useful in this story than an ability to translate ancient languages.

If I'd already written six full chapters, I'd be unwilling to make such a drastic change, but trying a different version of the step outline is easy. So I save the original, just in case, and start again.

1. Seb accidentally drops an exhibit in the museum while he is cleaning it. It opens and out falls a mobile phone or similar electronic device carefully wrapped in a special film that's kept it in remarkably pristine condition for something 200 years old.

2. Seb starts to take it to his boss but hesitates. This is worth a lot as scrap and it wouldn't really be stealing as no one else knew it existed.

3. He runs his fingers over the keys and is shocked to hear it bleep. How can it be working after all this time and why was it hidden in the first place? He wants to find out more about it so he takes it to Jane and asks her to try to make it go.

4. Jane won't do it. She'll get into trouble working on unauthorized electronics.

5. Seb persuades her to change her mind. (Don't know how yet.)

6. Jane gets the phone working and discovers it contains a different version of history from the one she's always believed was true. The elite who rule the world are ruthless – they are going to wipe out the ordinary population when they have outlived their usefulness.

7. Seb and Jane are determined to overthrow the elite. They set out to find others trying to do the same.

8. The elite realize they know too much and try to kill them.

9. Seb and Jane finally join with the others and take part in a rebellion.

10. The elite are overthrown.

Now I need to think much more about what Seb and Jane are actually going to do and, in order to do that, I'll need to work out more about them and the world in which they live. Step outlining is not a continuous process. It's interspersed with brainstorming sessions, character development, world building and thinking about the many other issues involved in creating a good story. But the step outline itself keeps those creative activities on track and lets us see how the story is developing.

12

Research

After I'd written the previous section on step outlining, I read it to my writers' group to test their reactions. One of the members works in a museum, and she immediately told me that artefacts are so carefully examined that anything hidden inside them would have already been found. In order for Seb to find a hidden device or message, it would need to be inside something that had only just been handed in or maybe something he discovers elsewhere. She also told me that many objects are handed to museums after the owner dies, so I'm now wondering whether Seb should be someone doing house clearance rather than a museum employee.

This sort of information from an expert can be invaluable when you're plotting. It not only prevents you making mistakes – it can also move your story in a different direction and make it much better. Most people love sharing what they know with a writer, and I often find that the information they provide triggers more ideas.

You may be wondering why I haven't suggested researching before you've come up with the basic idea for your story. Although it's perfectly possible to do that, I don't recommend it because it's easy to get so wrapped up in research at that stage that you never get around to writing the book. It's also a more effective use of your time to leave your research until you know what you need to find out.

The value of first-hand experience

Because we're writers, it's natural to turn to books and the internet when we're researching. The old saying is that a picture is worth a thousand words and, on that basis, a video is worth millions because it tells you even more. But it's always worth trying to experience things first-hand if you can as it will add extra authenticity to your writing. Books and videos can't give you the tiny details you need to bring your story alive: scents and sounds, tastes and feelings.

If you are writing a novel where your characters use horses as transport and you've never been on a horse, now is the time to try. Just one riding lesson will give you valuable background information on what it feels like to be on the back of such a large animal: how being higher lets you see further, how the horse moves his ears and head and how your body moves in time with his steps. But try to stay on board – it's safer to research what it feels like to fall off by talking to other people and reading books.

If you can't go to the place you are writing about because it's in the past or it's a complete figment of your imagination, try going somewhere similar. Living history museums can be a useful source of inspiration. It's so much easier to imagine life in a Saxon village when you've walked around one and explored its houses. Historical re-enactment and live action role play (LARPing) are also worth trying if they are relevant to your story. When I spent a LARPing weekend running through a wood battling goblins, I gained new insight into sword fighting and the meaning of phrases like "standing shoulder to shoulder" and "holding the line". Although the battles were fake, they felt surprisingly real so I also came away with a much better understanding of how soldiers feel when they go into battle.

In my experience, people are surprisingly co-operative with writers who want to experience things first-hand. As a result, I've been backstage at *Phantom of the Opera*, sat in on the pilot briefing for the Schneider Trophy and taken my advanced driving test. So if you think it would help your book if you got locked in a cell, went behind the scenes at a zoo or climbed the rigging of a tall ship, try asking. The worst that can happen is someone saying "no".

Research in action

To give you an example of the range of research that you could do for one book, here's a list of the research I did for *There Must Be Horses*.

- I read books on horse whispering and horse training.

- I spent a weekend watching horse trainer, Mark Rashid, demonstrate the way he helps horses overcome difficult behaviour. In the process, I met a troubled horse with a troubled background, who inspired me to create Meteor, the main horse in the book.

- I bought a horse so I could practise everything I'd learned. (Okay – that was going further than strictly necessary, but I had wanted a horse all my life and here was the perfect excuse.)

- I spent a day being the learner in an equine facilitated learning session. This gave me lots of ideas for the horse behaviour in the book as well as making me feel better about myself.

- I talked to a riding instructor about what goes wrong in riding lessons when someone pretends they can ride better than they really can.

- I read books about fostering and how children cope with loss, including a collection of interviews with young people who had been fostered. This added to the information I already had from being a foster parent myself in the past.

- I reread *Anne of Green Gables* by L M Montgomery, Jacqueline Wilson's books about Tracy Beaker and the first in Lauren Brooke's *Heartland* series to give me a better insight into the market I was aiming at. (It's always good to know your competition so you can make sure your book is different.)

13

Developing characters

As you work on your step outline, you'll start to see how you want your characters to behave, so you'll be able to develop them in more depth. And when you get to know them better, your characters will suggest further ways to develop the plot. That's why there's no real answer to the question "Which comes first: character or plot?" The two are so closely intertwined that it's impossible to separate them.

It's a good idea to keep a note of the decisions you make about each of your characters so you don't forget them. That will avoid Seb having blue eyes in chapter 2 and brown ones in chapter 22 or Jane being fearless with spiders in chapter 5 but terrified of them in chapter 35. However, if you decide to keep your records on one of those character development forms so popular with writing courses, don't feel you have to answer all the questions. Deciding facts about your characters too early can restrict your story choices later so it's best to leave your options open for as long as you can.

Age

One of the most important decisions to make about any character is their age, because how old we are affects the way we think, the way we behave and the way we relate to other people. That's partly because of the life experiences we've had, so when you decide on a character's age, count back from the date when the story is set, to see what was happening in the world while they were growing up. For example, if your novel is set in America in 1872, all but the very youngest characters would have been affected in some way by the Civil War.

Of course, this is more difficult if your story is set in the far future or a fantasy world. But it's still worth considering whether life has changed since they were small. In particular, if you're writing a post-apocalyptic novel, would any of your characters remember the major calamity that's happened?

Characters in their late teens are particularly useful in novels, even those not specifically aimed at young adults. Their lack of experience makes them look at the world with fresh eyes and gives them a desire to make sense of what's happening – both of which provide good opportunities for your readers to make sense of it too.

Gender

The gender of some of your characters will be determined by your plot. For instance, if you're writing a straight romance, you'll definitely need a man and a woman. However, you may have more flexibility with other characters and storylines, especially now most jobs are open to both men and women. But before you make your decision, give some thought to the personal pronouns *he* and *she*.

When you use them in your book, it's important that your readers know which character they refer to, and they'll find that easier if the people in a scene aren't all the same gender. Don't become so pedantic about this that you ruin your story, but it's worth keeping in mind when you are thinking up minor characters.

Names

Names are far more important to me than appearance. I find that my characters never come completely alive until I know what they're called. But I need to choose their names carefully because I find it hard to change them after I've started creating the story.

Names can come from a variety of places. Elisabeth Beresford's Wombles share their names with rivers and other places around the world, J M Barrie invented Wendy for *Peter Pan* and J K Rowling used an old-fashioned word for bumblebee to create Dumbledore. Whatever my inspiration, I always try to make each character's name start with a different letter of the alphabet. This avoids confusion and helps those who want to skim-read the names. For similar reasons, I avoid names that look very similar unless there's a good reason. So I might use Harry or Barry but never both together unless I'm trying to be funny.

Before you make a firm decision, try saying your potential choices aloud to give you a feel for how they sound and whether they fit your character. Also try them with other names that are likely to occur together. That's particularly important when you're choosing names for a romantic couple or a surname to go with a first name – some name pairs have a pleasant rhythm and others don't.

Using real names

Unless you are writing an historical novel featuring characters who really existed, it's best to avoid names of real people. Obviously it's possible to pick on a real name by mistake, and most people won't mind being connected with a hero. However, their reaction may be less welcoming if they share their name with the villain, especially if they also share the same profession. So, if you want to include a dishonest lawyer or an incompetent doctor in your book, check as carefully as you can that there isn't a real lawyer or doctor with the same name. Professional organizations can be a big help here.

I never realized the importance of this issue until it happened to me. I was reading a book about parenting children with special needs when one of the fictitious sample families turned out to have the same surname as me. Not only that, they had two boys with a chronic illness, just like I had. The only difference between the two families was that the sample one was cracking under the strain and mine wasn't. I was surprised how strongly I reacted to what I hope was an innocent coincidence. It felt very personal and, although I didn't complain to the author, I was tempted to name a villain after her on a tit-for-tat basis.

I always play safe and do internet searches for my characters' names. This isn't just to rule out the issue above; it's to make sure that I haven't accidentally named my heroine after a porn star or invented a name that has a rude meaning. Obviously I have to be extra careful with this when writing for young readers but, whatever the age of your target audience, a few minutes spent checking can avoid embarrassing mistakes.

Appearance

Although behaviour is more important than appearance, knowing what your characters look like can help them come alive in your head. Some people use photos of people from magazines or the internet to remind them what their characters look like. Others prefer to think which actor they would cast to play them in the movie version. Another alternative is to think of someone that you know, but be careful if you do this as they may not be happy if they recognize themselves in your book.

Personally, I prefer to rely on a mental image rather than a physical one and it's often very vague. I once co-wrote a radio script with my son that featured a talking horse and, when we had finished, we discovered the horse in my head was white while the one in his head was black. That hadn't affected our ability to write the story because the colour of the horse didn't matter.

Although a detailed description of each character's appearance may help you write about them, that doesn't mean you have to provide the entire description to your readers. They will develop a mental image of what your characters look like as soon as they read about them, whether you provide a description or not. So, if there is something about a character's appearance that is crucial to the plot, it's important that you mention it as soon as possible before the picture in your readers' heads becomes too fixed.

For instance, if the final crisis in your story is going to be solved by a character called Katy escaping through a tiny window, you need to establish early on that she's small and agile. It's no good waiting until she's trapped before you mention her size because, by then, your readers will have decided what she looks like. If they've always imagined Katy as tall, they won't appreciate being told they are wrong and they'll have trouble believing the rest of the story.

With something as important as this, it's often best to reveal it as part of a scene rather than just mention it in passing so that readers will be more likely to remember it. Maybe Katy has to stand on tiptoe to reach a shelf, she's teased about her size or she has to look up to see another character's face.

Backstory

We are all shaped by the events that happen to us, and these events make up what are called our backstories. Each of your characters will have their own backstory, but neither you nor your readers need to know everything that's happened in them. The events that matter are the ones that shaped your character in ways that are significant to your story. So the fact that a character nearly drowned when he was twelve is important if it left him terrified of travelling by ship and the plot includes a sea crossing. But the same fact doesn't matter if it's only effect was to make him learn to swim, and he won't be required to do that in the story.

Although it's important to tell your readers important facts about your character's appearance early in the story, the same is not true of their backstory. In fact, one of the major reasons for a book taking too long to get going is including too much backstory long before your reader needs to know it. On the other hand, you don't want to hold back some information too long either. If you wait until your hero has been shipwrecked before you reveal that she was the high school swimming champion, that skill will look too conveniently contrived to be believable.

The right solution is to drip-feed the vital backstory information into your story a bit at a time. Less important information can be left out completely or included just to make it harder for readers to realize what really matters. You can also put questions in your readers' heads by hinting that important information exists without revealing it completely. If this awakens their curiosity enough, their desire to learn the truth will help to keep them reading.

Family issues

Family ties make a big difference to how characters react to situations. James Bond's approach to danger and casual sex would probably be quite different if he had a loving wife and three children waiting for him at home. That's why so many detectives, spies and adventurers in stories are single, divorced or otherwise free of relatives and family ties. It gives them the freedom to behave any way they like without fear of repercussions on the people they love.

However, family ties don't always have bad effects on stories. The complex relationships in families form the basis of many successful plots, and they add an emotional depth to countless others. You can use them to give your characters the motivation they need to escape from danger, the determination to dive back into the burning building to rescue the people they love or, when disaster strikes, a reason to seek revenge.

You don't need to work out your character's complete family tree. Concentrate on the relationships that matter to your story: the older sister who keeps trying to marry off your bachelor detective, the ageing mother whose needs conflict with your character's career plans or the talented brother who overshadows your character's own achievements. As always, you don't need to decide all of this at the beginning. You can decide on relatives as and when you need them and, where necessary, adjust the plot to introduce them earlier.

The problem with parents

Good parents love their children and try to keep them safe. As a result, they stop them doing anything that might turn into an adventure and, when the children do get into trouble, they rush in and solve their problems for them – a situation guaranteed to produce an unsatisfactory ending. So, if an important character in your story is a child or teenager, you may find it helpful to get rid of their parents.

That's why so many main characters in children's books are orphans. However, killing off parents is a drastic step and best done well before the start of your story unless you want to focus on grief. Making parents workaholics is less gruesome and more realistic in the present day when people often work long hours but rarely die young. Boarding schools are handy too, and so is setting your story back in time to a period when 12 year olds were considered adults. I don't recommend making the parents go on holiday and forget to take their child with them – it's been done so thoroughly in the *Home Alone* movies that it doesn't look original any more. But the family might get separated in some other way, especially if there's a war, a tsunami or some other disaster.

14

Making characters believable

Have you ever read a book or watched a movie where a character acts in a way you can't believe? If so, you'll remember how annoying it was and how much it affected your opinion of the story. To make sure that you never annoy your readers in that way, you need to create your characters skilfully so the way you need them to behave seems natural. That's why it's best not to decide too much about them until you know the part they will play in your story. Delaying decisions until you can see the effect they will have leaves you free to develop both the character and the plot in the best way possible. If necessary, you can then go back through your plot and adjust earlier steps to incorporate that decision.

Providing information in good time

As I mentioned in the section on backstory, if we don't let the readers know that a character has a vital skill until he uses it, they are likely to decide that's unbelievable and only put in to get the author out of a plot hole. So it's important that we give our readers this information earlier in the story and, because it's so crucial, it's best to mention it more than once just in case they miss it the first time. But we don't want to make the mentions too obvious in case they telegraph the ending by giving too big a hint of what's to come.

Let's go back to the example I used earlier of someone who used to be the high school swimming champion. An obvious way to bring that into the story is to show her swimming, but here are some ways you could let readers know about her achievement without her getting wet.

- Make her grumble that getting up early in the morning reminds her of all the early starts to swimming practise when she was at school.

- Make her angry with her dad for pushing her so hard to be a champion swimmer when it wasn't what she wanted.

- Make her sister tired of always playing second best because she wasn't a championship swimmer.

- Show her struggling with something else (maths, reading, woodwork) and boasting of her swimming achievement as a way to show she's not a total failure.

In each case, the reader is likely to focus on the emotion of the situation and not realize your ulterior motive in making her a good swimmer until it becomes crucial to the plot.

Of course, there are some stories where we deliberately keep a fact secret from the reader for most of the story. This applies to many murder mysteries and to any plot with a twist at the end. But even then, the reader should be able to go back through the story and find hints that point towards the twist that are so subtle that they either missed them completely or misunderstood them the first time around. The movie *The Sixth Sense* does this brilliantly. When you finally meet the final twist at the end (which I'm not going to give away here), everything suddenly clicks into place and tiny things you didn't quite understand become totally clear. It's worth watching twice just to see how it's done.

Motivation matters

Sometimes it's not a skill or the lack of it that's the problem. It's the way a character reacts to a situation that doesn't feel right. Motivation matters, so readers will only believe that a person acts in a particular way if they understand the reasons for that behaviour. For instance, if you want a normally polite character to be rude to someone, you need to show that she's had a really bad morning that's driven her to breaking point or that she's finally snapped because the recipient of the rudeness has been picking on her for weeks.

Solving motivation problems often involves doing more character development. When I was creating *There Must Be Horses*, I knew Sasha wanted to stay at her new foster home, but I also knew that the story needed her foster parents to refuse to keep her permanently. However, they were such a naturally kind couple that the story would only be believable if there was a reason for them to turn Sasha away. It took me a long time and many false starts to find one that was strong enough to make the book work, and I only managed it when I worked out a backstory for the foster parents that explained how they felt. That reason then became pivotal to the whole story, and I made Sasha go through the same search I had to discover why she couldn't stay.

15

Character arcs

A feature of many successful stories is known in story jargon as a positive character arc: a change for the good in a character during a story. That change can take many forms but, in order for it to be successful, it has to be one that the readers find satisfying and believable. Common character arcs include:

- a timid man overcomes his fear enough to do something brave.

- an ambitious woman gives up her chance of success in order to help someone else.

- a selfish man ends up caring enough about someone else to risk his life for them.

- a shy girl overcomes her fear of speaking in public in order to lead a campaign against injustice.

- a villain sees the error of his ways and lets his captives go.

Some stories contain negative story arcs where a character gradually becomes worse and worse. That's okay if it's the villain who is deteriorating, but books where the hero changes from good to bad tend to be downbeat and depressing unless he eventually learns the error of his ways and improves. That doesn't mean you shouldn't write that sort of story, but it's not an easy task. You'll have to work hard to keep your readers caring about someone who is becoming increasingly unpleasant.

Character arcs are not essential

Although an interesting character arc can improve your plot, you don't have to have one. In most detective series, police procedurals and superhero adventures, the main character stays much the same throughout each book. And readers like it that way. They read book after book because they like that character so they don't want them to change.

16

Character development in action

Let's go back to the story we started earlier about Seb and Jane. I've decided that the idea of any piece of electronics still working two hundred years later is too hard to believe. So the message Seb finds is now a diary written in a language he doesn't know (probably French), and Jane has gone back to being a language expert. That means the current step outline is:

1. Seb is demolishing an empty house when he finds an old diary hidden under the floorboards, but he can't understand what it says.

2. Seb starts to take it to his boss but hesitates. Taking it wouldn't really be stealing because no one else knows it exists. Money is tight, and this might be valuable to a collector. But it's hard to know how much it's worth without knowing what it says.

3. He takes the diary to Jane and asks her to translate it.

4. Jane won't do it. The study of history is strictly controlled, and she'll get into trouble if she works on an unauthorized artefact.

5. Seb persuades her to change her mind by tempting her to tackle something new instead of the dry, approved texts she usually has to translate. Jane agrees reluctantly, worried she'll be caught and get into trouble.

6. Jane starts to translate the diary and quickly discovers that it contains a different version of history from the one she's always been told was true. The elite hold power by force, keep the ordinary population in ignorance and kill unwanted members of the population without a qualm if they cause trouble or are no longer useful.

7. Seb and Jane are determined to overthrow the elite. They set out to find others trying to do the same.

8. The elite realize they know too much and try to kill them.

9. Seb and Jane finally join with the others and take part in a rebellion.

10. The elite are overthrown.

Now we know all that, let's think about our characters in more depth. Jane's surname is Knox because it popped into my head by itself and feels right. (It's often best to go with your gut feelings on issues like names.) She's in her early twenties, which makes her old enough to have the qualifications and experience she needs for her job. Her whole life has been orthodox – standard education followed by a civil service job at the museum – so she's always followed the rules. This sets her up to have a character arc by letting her become more willing to challenge authority as the story progresses. However, I'm tempted to show a small sign of rebellion early on by making her ability with French the result of some unapproved study in addition to her official course. (I'll decide on that later.) My mental image of her is short and dark, but so far her appearance doesn't matter much.

Seb Stone is also in his early twenties, and he's a bit of a geek with a flair for electronics and everything mechanical. I imagine him as scruffy with straggly blond hair, although his appearance isn't relevant to the story yet. He's self-taught with no formal qualifications, but he has established a reputation for himself as someone who can make things work. He earns a somewhat precarious living doing odd jobs for local people with a bit of buying and selling on the side that sometimes takes him to the edge of legality. This makes him very different from Jane which opens up the possibility of conflict between them. His edgy lifestyle also provides him with experience and contacts that may come in handy later in the story.

17

Sorting out the setting

As you work on your plot, you'll find you need to know more about your setting. As with characters, it's best to develop this while you are working out the story so you only worry about the details that matter.

Period

The time period in which your story takes place is an important component of the setting. At its most basic, you have to choose whether it's going to happen in the past, the present or the future. (Although, if you're writing about time travel, it could be all three.) Then, if you've chosen the past, you have to decide on the exact period you want to write about. It's important to pick a time that interests you because you're going to have to do lots of research to make sure all the facts are right. Even small inaccuracies can jar with readers, pulling them out of the story, and making them less likely to recommend your book to their friends.

If you can't cope with that amount of research, consider using a fantasy or alternative reality setting instead. That can be very similar to the historical period that interests you, but you don't have to worry about getting every detail correct. It will also give you the freedom to change anything about the real history that will make your plot work better.

If you are setting your book in the future, you can give your imagination free-rein, provided you stay within the boundaries of believability. Readers will find it easy to accept that civilization has collapsed after an apocalyptic event or that technology has advanced to amazing new levels, but they will struggle to believe that Earth's gravity has disappeared or trees have turned blue. If blue trees are vital to your story, move your setting to another planet or a fantasy world where such things are possible.

Place

The second component of setting is the place or places where your story will happen. Using a real place sounds as if it could save you lots of work. You don't have to make anything up because it's all decided for you: from street layout to public transport to the position of hotels and schools. And that's where the problems start. Using a real place gives you no leeway to make things the way you need them to be for the story. However much you want your hero to be mugged in a quiet alleyway next to the library, you can't do that if there isn't an alleyway there. Plus the real businesses in the area may not be too happy about being featured in a story that puts them in a bad light, so you may have trouble finding a suitable bar where drug dealers can sell their wares or a warehouse for a mass murderer to use to dispose of the bodies.

Another snag with using real places is that your readers may know them better than you do. Unless you live in the place yourself or your research is perfect, you'll probably get letters from fans pointing out that the number 52 bus doesn't run on Sundays or the hotel to the right of the police station closed down in 2010, so it wasn't possible for the murderer to stay there in 2016.

Despite all these problems, there are some stories where it's essential to use a real place as a setting for at least some of the scenes. If yours is one of them, arm yourself with up-to-date maps and timetables, guidebooks and photos for easy reference. YouTube is definitely your friend for this type of research as personal videos often contain the small details you don't find in a travel documentary.

Of course, it's best if you can visit the place yourself and walk around the streets your characters will use. If that's not possible, try to find someone who lives there who is willing to help with the small but important details you can't find elsewhere. Other authors can be particularly helpful because they understand the problem — try putting a request on author discussion groups to find someone suitable.

Inventing a place

If you're going to invent the place where your story takes place, it makes sense to base it on somewhere that really exists. That gives you all the advantages of using a real place with none of the disadvantages. You can use the real place as a starting point to help you create a picture of the place in your head, but change as many details as necessary to make your story work the way you want it to.

I often combine several places together to create my settings. The palace in my Pony-Mad Princess series is based on a mixture of Windsor Castle and Osborne House (Queen Victoria's home on the Isle of Wight) while the grounds are a blend of Windsor Great Park and Ross-on-Wye. In that series, the palace is in another country that I never name, but you may prefer to put your imaginary town in Colorado or Wales or some other part of the world that fits your story. Although doing that will involve a bit of research, it can help your readers create the setting in their heads.

Inventing worlds

If you're writing fantasy or science fiction, you'll need to invent more than just a town. You've got to create a whole world or universe and at least one civilization. World building is such a big topic that people have written whole books about how to do it. It's also fun so, unless you are firm with yourself, it can easily take over all your writing time and maybe your whole life. (A bit like me buying myself a horse.)

To stop that happening, it's best to restrict yourself to the aspects of your world that are important to the story. You don't need to work out all the details of a new religion that you only mention in passing, and, if you need someone to speak an unknown language, you can just create a few essential words (yes, no, hello, etc). There's no need to copy Tolkien's efforts with Elvish and invent a complete vocabulary and grammar.

To speed up the world-building process, you can start with real facts and places and work from there. Many sword and sorcery fantasies use the Middle Ages as a starting point while Michelle Paver's *Chronicles of Ancient Darkness* goes farther back and weaves a story about prehistoric hunter-gatherers in a world where magic and the supernatural are real.

Maps and records

As you create your setting, you need to keep a record of what you decide so you can avoid mistakes later. I used to resist drawing maps and diagrams because I'd seen those detailed maps authors put at the front of their fantasy novels and I didn't feel up to producing one. But I soon discovered that quick sketches help me remember information about my setting far easier than copious notes. Mine aren't artistic – scrappy scrawls are quite good enough as no one sees them except me.

If you're using a real place, you can buy maps instead of drawing your own. But even then, you'll need to draw plans of important buildings showing where the different rooms are and you may need to plan the position of doors, windows and furniture in individual rooms which feature in any action scenes. These drawings can be quite bare at first – just rough outlines – leaving you free to add details as you need them, and to make any changes that prove necessary.

18

Setting in action

Let's go back to *Future Proof* and develop the setting where Jane and Seb are having their adventures. So far, all we know is that it's a small town with a museum. I've abandoned the idea of a university for the time being as that would make the town too big and probably mean too much help was available close by. I can always put one in later if I decide I need it, but, even if I do, it might be better to have it somewhere else so Seb and Jane have to travel to get there – a journey that could provide extra problems for them to overcome.

It's tempting to put the town in the USA, because that's a common setting for books of this type. However, I've never been there so it would take masses of research to try to get everything right and, even then, I would probably make mistakes which would get picked up by keen-eyed American readers. So I'm going to play safe and set my small town in the south of England because that's the part of the world I know best. It will also allow me to take my characters to some real places if I want to. London is an obvious choice, but I also have a fancy to involve Bletchley Park – the home of the code breakers who helped the allies win World War II.

Of course, this is the future so England won't be quite the same as it is now. That removes some of the need for accuracy, but I'm still going to play safe and minimize the need for research by creating an imaginary town called Deston. A quick Google search showed me this is as safe choice as there are no real places with the same name. I was also delighted to find that Deston is a French name meaning destiny. I love it when things like that happen by accident – it's s usually a sign that I'm heading in the right direction.

I'm basing Deston on a typical English country town close to where I live, so my imaginary town currently has an old town hall that's been turned into the museum, a market square beside the main church and a river with a bridge over it. I may change a few of those details as the plot progresses, and I'm sure to add some more.

Sorting out the world

The whole plot for *Future Proof* pivots on the information that Seb and Jane have discovered about the changes that have been made to history. But I haven't just got to decide what they are. I've also got to work out how this society works, how the elite run it and what consequences that has for Seb and Jane.

There's been a gap of several days between writing this section and the last one and during that gap I've been running ideas through my head all the time. That's caused a burned dinner or two because I often think best when I'm doing something else. But it's also got the story a bit clearer in my mind.

One thing I'm now sure about is that ordinary people only know an incorrect version of history taught in schools and at museums like the one where Jane works. In order for that to work, there mustn't be any living memories of the world as it really was, so enough time must have passed since history was changed for everyone alive then to have grown old and died. On the other hand, it seems better not to set the story further in the future than absolutely necessary because it would be convenient to have some of the same buildings around. So 1,000 years in the future is too far and 50 years isn't enough. I've settled on 200 years as a first try, but I'll change that later if it causes problems.

If the current growth in population continues until then, Deston will be very crowded, which will add complications to the story that I don't want. To deal with that, I've decided that something's happened to make the population fall. I'm not sure that a cataclysmic event like a plague will fit with my story, but a falling birthrate could work. Maybe the elite are controlling how many babies are born – they certainly wouldn't want too big a population, using up natural resources and becoming harder to control. I'll decide for sure later, but I definitely like the idea of having fewer people around as there will be plenty of disused buildings and deserted places that might prove useful.

The elite are dictators so they have removed any mention of democracy from history to prevent the population realizing there's an alternative way of organizing society. However, there will be other facts missing too, including the original situation that brought the elite to power and who the elite actually are. After more thought, I've come back to my original idea that this was going to be a story about an alien invasion. I abandoned that earlier because I didn't want it to be a war story, but I like the idea of a secret alien takeover of the world. That's as far as I've got at this stage. It's just the bare bones, but it's enough to let me move on with the plotting process. I can add more details as the story develops.

The effect on the plot

The story that started off as a fairly standard (and possibly funny) alien invasion with battling spaceships now looks as if it's going to be a science fiction thriller with political overtones, set in a dystopian future. That's not a problem: we're only at the plotting stage so changes are easy to make. The story is also showing signs of some deep themes – freedom, democracy and courage – which is great because deep themes often produce good books. A plot that runs on more than one level is much more satisfying for readers than one that's shallow and superficial.

19

Making your story original

We all grow up with stories and, as we watch, read and listen, we store the details away in our memories. As a result, it's not surprising that some of those details resurface as ideas when we start to create stories of our own. There is no shame in that. It's perfectly natural, and it's a valid source of inspiration because there is no copyright in ideas. Copyright only applies to the expression of those ideas.

However, it isn't okay to regurgitate someone else's complete story and call it your own. That's plagiarism. So, if you're inspired by themes and ideas from stories you've read, make sure you develop them in different ways so your story is different from the sources of your inspiration. That won't just free you from accusations of plagiarism – it will also please your readers as they want a story that's as original as possible.

But being original can be difficult. According to the story analysts, there are only a limited number of basic storylines in the world. They disagree on what that number is, but what matters is that it's virtually impossible to create a new story that has no similarity at all to any other story that's ever been written before. Plus, some genres have a basic plot structure that readers want to see – for example, a romance usually has boy-meets-girl, boy-breaks-up-with-girl and boy-and-girl-get-back-together. It's the way those events happen that make your story different from others of the same type.

One way to ensure originality is to never accept the first idea that pops into your head. In my experience, that's the one that's most likely to have come from another story you have read or watched. So always brainstorm several ideas before you make a decision: it's often one of the later ones that proves to be best.

If you do spot a worrying similarity to another book or movie, check carefully to see exactly what the similarities are.

- Is your setting very similar to the one in the other book?

- Are your characters like those in the other book?

- Do they use any of the same methods as the other characters to try to overcome their problem?

- In a detective story, are any of the clues too similar?

- Is your ending the same as the other book?

Then change your plot to take those similarities away. There's a high chance that you'll make your story better in the process, because you'll have given it more thought.

Putting the search for originality into action

I love science fiction and dystopian fantasies about repressive regimes, so I have plenty of ideas in my head that might creep into *Future Proof*. As a result, I've got to be alert for any tendency to slide into someone else's plot by mistake. For example, one reason that I've opted for Seb to find a written message rather than a video is because I want to avoid any similarity to the importance of films in the TV series, *The Man in the High Castle*. The other is that I'm sceptical about whether the technology could have lasted for as long as it would need to.

The idea of alien invaders disguised as humans is definitely not original. It has so much story potential that it often crops up in science fiction and is a major component of at least one well-known conspiracy theory. That doesn't mean I can't use it, but it does mean I have to be careful to keep my aliens different from the ones in other stories. In particular, I need an original way to spot the difference between aliens and genuine humans. Definitely not flatulence (already used to good comedic effect in *Doctor Who*) or crooked little fingers (used in the classic TV series *The Invaders*). At the moment, I'm thinking of making my aliens tall and slim with long, elegant fingers that look human but are sufficiently distinctive to mark their owners as part of the elite.

Faced with an unpleasant dictatorship, it's logical to suppose that there will be resistance to them, so some sort of rebellion or rebel force is a common feature of many dystopian novels. It's such a basic idea that including rebels in *Future Proof* doesn't mean I'm stealing other people's ideas any more than a romance writer is stealing ideas if they make a boy and girl fall in love.

However, I don't want to make my rebels overcome the elite by being superior fighters. It's too obvious, too easy and, given Seb and Jane's background, it's going to be hard to make believable. As I'm not interested in creating huge action sequences, I'd prefer to make my characters reach their goal in a more imaginative way than just brute force. Two sayings are running through my head that may provide inspiration eventually. One is a verse by William Blake which I am free to use because it's out of copyright. It says:

> *Rise, like lions after slumber*
> *In unvanquishable number!*
> *Shake your chains to earth like dew*
> *Which in sleep had fallen on you:*
> *Ye are many—they are few!*

The other is the phrase *speak truth to power* which comes from the Quaker tradition of trying to solve problems without violence. It fits well with the storyline so far: Jane's found truth in that diary and she's somehow going to use that truth to change the world.

With all those thoughts in mind, here's a revised step outline.

1. Seb is demolishing an empty house when he finds an old diary (or maybe a time capsule containing the diary and other things) hidden in a wall. It's in a language he doesn't understand so he can't read it.

2. Seb starts to take it to his boss but hesitates. Taking it wouldn't really be stealing because no one else knows it exists. Money is tight and this might be valuable to a collector. But it's hard to know how much it's worth without knowing what it says.

3. He takes the diary to Jane and asks her to translate it.

4. Jane won't do it. The study of history is strictly controlled and she'll get into trouble if she works on an unauthorized artefact.

5. Seb persuades her to change her mind by tempting her to discover some real history – not just the dull approximation that's taught in schools. Jane agrees, although she is still worried she'll be caught and get into trouble.

6. Jane starts to translate the diary and quickly discovers that it contains a different version of history from the one she's always been told was true. The elite are the descendants of alien invaders who took power by force. They keep the ordinary population in ignorance and poverty and kill them without hesitation if the need arises.

7. Seb and Jane are determined to overthrow the elite. They set out to find others trying to do the same.

8. The elite realize they know too much and try to kill them.

9. Seb and Jane finally join with the others and take part in a rebellion.

10. The elite are overthrown.

Some of those steps are becoming so clear in my head that I could start writing them. But I'm not going to yet because my ideas may change as I develop the rest of the story.

20

Adding humour

Even if you're not trying to write a funny book, you may like to follow the example set by Shakespeare and include a touch of comedy to lighten the mood of an otherwise serious story. This isn't compulsory, but it can provide a welcome break for readers from otherwise never-ending tension and make painful topics easier to write about. Also, making your reader smile or laugh increases the impact when you build the tension back up again because they experience a larger emotional swing.

Adding humour to your story doesn't involve creating strings of jokes. To make it work well and fit in with the story, the humour needs to come from the characters themselves: what they say, what they do and how they react to each other and to the events around them. Sometimes those events are funny in their own right but, with the right characters, even a tragic situation like going over the top from the trenches can raise a smile. (If you don't believe me, watch the final episode of *Blackadder Goes Forth*.)

The important thing to understand is that good comedy characters never realize they are funny. They are just being themselves and that makes them act in ways we find amusing. Although audiences roar with laughter at the antics of Mr Bean, he never laughs at himself – he is very serious all the time.

Funny characters usually have at least one strong characteristic that defines them and gets them into trouble. Buddy, the human reared as an elf in *Elf*, delights audiences because he is totally naïve – a child in an adult's body – while Bart Simpson is a mischievous rebel with no respect for authority.

If you want to create a comedy character, try to think of that defining characteristic first. Think how that is going to affect what they do and say and then build their character around that. Maybe they have a phrase they often say, something that always worries them or something they always want to have with them. Once your readers have grown accustomed to that, they'll always be expecting it and will like it when it happens at inappropriate times.

If you create a group of people with different characteristics, you can make them bounce off each other in amusing ways. (You can see this in action in any episode of your favourite sitcom.) But they don't all have to be funny characters. It's a good idea to include at least one fairly ordinary person in the mix as this creates even more opportunities for humour. That's why comedy double acts are often made up of a funny guy and a straight one – Laurel and Hardy are a classic example.

The woolly characters in my *Alien Sheep* are just such a group. Although they are identical in appearance and numbered rather than named, I made each one have his own characteristic. Two is obsessed with autograph hunting, Three has no sense of humour and Six is a worrier. My personal favourite is Eight, who believes everything he is told, and bursts into tears every time he learns that a story isn't true. Once I had created this mix of characters, the dialogue for the flock flowed naturally because I could easily imagine what each of them would say in any situation.

Future Proof is a thriller rather than a comedy, but it doesn't have to be miserable. The contrast between Seb's easy-going attitude to life and Jane's serious upbringing will offer good opportunities to add some humour if I want to. In addition, some of the minor characters they meet could be designed to raise a smile from our readers.

21

Special issues with series

I've put this section here because it's often at this stage of the plotting process that you start to wonder if your story has the potential to become a series. That's definitely happening to me with *Future Proof* because I'm not sure I can make Seb and Jane save mankind in one normal length book without making the plot too simplistic and trite. A series of three books would give me the space to give the story more depth.

The pros and cons of series

Writing a series makes marketing easier because, once you've hooked your readers with one book, they are likely to want to read the others. This works so well that publishers sometimes sell the first book really cheaply in order to bring readers in.

Another advantage is that you can use the same basic idea, characters and setting for the whole series. Unfortunately this is a disadvantage too, because writing about the same characters over and over again can be boring. And once the first book is published, you'll be tied into the decisions you made for that one so you'll have less freedom when you plot the later stories. So, before you commit yourself to writing a series, make sure you are sufficiently excited by the central idea to want to write several books about it.

Freestanding series

In this type of series, each book is completely freestanding with a plot that's independent of the others. As the series progresses, the main characters either remain much the same or change only slightly, and any serial storyline that runs from book to book is so minor that the books can be read in any order without causing problems to the reader. Series about detectives, spies or superheroes usually fit into this category. So do my *Pony-Mad Princess* books.

Because this type of series is open-ended, you can test the market with one or more books and add new ones for as long as you wish. With *The Pony-Mad Princess*, I started with six books and added new ones in response to demand from readers. I've now written thirteen and I would find it hard to add another because I've used up so many storylines already.

To develop a free-standing series, you need to think of a setting with plenty of potential for different storylines. It helps to choose a place where a variety of scenarios are likely to arise naturally. A desert island with a population of two offers very few storylines, but police stations have much more potential, as do hospitals, vets, hotels, schools and any other place that has contact with the public. They allow you to have new people coming in for each book, bringing new stories with them.

Into that setting, you need to put at least one strong main character who will feature in every story. It's a good idea to have some other slightly less important regulars as well to provide someone for your main character to talk to: Superman has Lois Lane and many detectives have an assistant. But resist having too many as the more you have, the more complicated the plotting becomes and the harder it is for your readers to remember who's who.

Once you've developed the basic concept, check that the series has enough potential by writing brief outlines for three or more books. They don't have to be very long – you only need to jot down the central storyline in one or two paragraphs. If you can do this and you are still excited by the idea, the series is worth developing further. If you can't think of enough ideas or you feel terminally bored, you need to move on to a different project.

Freestanding series without regular characters

There are exceptions to every rule so there are some freestanding series that don't have the same main characters in every book: it's the setting that links them together. Two examples that spring to mind are *The Chronicles of Narnia* by C S Lewis and the Discworld novels by Terry Pratchett. But both of those series do have strong characters who turn up often enough to become well-known to readers.

Series that tell a story

The second type of series has a major overarching storyline that develops a bit more in each book and culminates in the last one. To work well, each individual book needs to contain a complete well-paced plot of its own which develops the main storyline and contains at least one sub-plot or story strand that is told completely in that book. So, at the end of each book, the reader finds a satisfactory end to that episode as well as the desire to read the next book to find out what happens next.

These series don't go on forever – they contain a finite number of books – and they are best read in the correct order. Trilogies like Tolkien's *The Lord of the Rings* and Philip Pullman's *His Dark Materials* fall into this category. So will *Future Proof* if I decide to turn it into a series.

The techniques for developing this type of series are the same as for single novels, but the storyline and characterization need to be very strong in order to hold your readers' attention. It's sensible to work out the overarching plot for the whole series before you start working on the details for each individual book. This is particularly important if you are following the usual practice of publishing the books one at a time, because you can't go back and change a story that's already been published in order to sort out a plot problem in a later one.

In less skilfully written series, the individual books don't contain complete stories – they are just sections of the main story that end on a cliffhanger designed to sell the next book without offering the reader any completion at all. This type of series is really just a long book cut into pieces. It risks leaving readers feeling cheated which, in turn, increases the chances of bad reviews. But don't panic if you've just realized your current project fits into that last category. You can increase your chances of pleasing your readers by doing some careful plotting to give each individual book a satisfactory ending.

Keeping the reader up to date

When magazines print serials, they start each episode with a "story so far" section. TV serials often use a montage of shots during the credits to get over the same information. Neither method works well in book series: they look clunky and they can turn the reader off. But you still need to give new readers the information they need to understand what's happening while not boring those who have already read the previous books.

The skill here is to sort out which information is essential and work it into the story as naturally as possible. It's best to feed it in a little at a time rather than put it all in one big chunk (or infodump) near the beginning. Exactly how you decide to do that is part of the writing process rather than plotting, but I'm mentioning it here so you can bear it in mind while you are planning your books.

Putting series planning into action

As I mentioned at the beginning of this chapter, I am considering turning the plot of *Future Proof* into a three-book series. Three is a good number as it allows us to use the classic rule of three technique – try once and fail, try again and fail, try again and succeed. But Seb and Jane need to achieve enough in each book to keep the reader hopeful that they will succeed eventually. So the endings of books 1 and 2 wouldn't be total failures. They would be like those situations where you are climbing a hill and reach what you think is the top, only to discover that there is more climbing ahead that you couldn't see before. Walkers and climbers sometimes refer to this as reaching a false summit, and that's what I need to provide for my readers.

Once Seb and Jane realize the importance of the diary, they're going to want help and that's likely to involve trying to get in touch with others who want to rebel against the elite. So one false summit could be finally reaching the people they hope are going to help them only to discover that they are fake, dead, imaginary or nearly as bad as the elite themselves. Something also needs to happen then to heighten Jane and Seb's resolve, help them overcome their disappointment and make them (and the readers) determined to continue their search for help.

For the moment, I'm going to continue working on the whole plot and leave the decision about whether it will be a single book or a series until I see how it turns out. Then, if I decide on a trilogy, I can go through my step outline, find the best places for the false summits and build them up to be satisfactory endings for the first two books.

22

Viewpoint

There are many ways to write a story. Putting *Future Proof* to one side for a moment, here's a piece I've written about evacuees in World War II.

The arrival of the train caused a flurry of activity on the crowded platform. Teachers scurried around through the billowing smoke, trying to organize the children onto the right carriages. Most didn't want to go – they clung to their mothers and cried. But one or two went on board so willingly that the teachers wondered how bad home must be for them to be so eager to leave it behind.

In the midst of this activity, the Spike children stood together, holding hands while their mother wiped their noses, checked their gas masks and tried to imprint their faces on her brain forever. She couldn't afford photographs. These memories would be all she had to remember them until the war was over. Daisy, the eldest, knew that too but the others were too young to understand how long they might be apart. Edward was sure he'd be home for Christmas and Elsie had no concept of time at all.

I've written those two paragraphs as if I'm watching what is happening without being involved in it. I mention what Mum is thinking and what Daisy knew, but I'm not looking at the scene through their eyes. Creative writing teachers call this author's view, God's eye view, omniscient viewpoint or, if they are really keen on jargon, third person omniscient viewpoint. This is much less popular than it used to be and can be heavy going for the reader if you use it for an entire novel. However, you may find it useful for some parts of your story.

Now here's the same scene again written in a different way.

Daisy held tight to Edward and Elsie as the train puffed into the station, breathing smoke like a dragon. She'd never been in such a crowd before or seen her teachers in such a state. She'd also never seen so many women and children crying. Was this what war was all about – families being ripped apart? Dad had already gone and now it was their turn.

She ducked her head as Mum tried to wipe her nose. She didn't need it. She was too old for that sort of mothering, and she wasn't crying – not outwardly anyway. She could feel a pit of loneliness growing inside her, but she tried not to let it show. She had to be strong like Mum, because she was going to have to take Mum's place in their new home. And if she got upset now, so would Elsie and that would mean her little sister travelling the whole way in wet knickers.

This time I'm watching the scene through Daisy's eyes. I'm inside her head so I see only what she sees and I know only what she knows. So I talk about how Daisy feels, but I don't mention anything that's going on in Mum's head. I'm writing in the third person because I refer to Daisy as *she*, and creative writing teachers call this viewpoint third person close or third person immediate.

Here's my third and final attempt at the scene in the station.

I hold tight to Edward and Elsie as the train puffs into the station, breathing smoke like a dragon. I've never been in such a crowd before and nearly all the women and children are crying. Even my teachers look upset. Is this what war is all about – families being ripped apart? Dad left last week and now it's our turn to go.

I duck my head as Mum tries to wipe my nose. I hate it when she does that. I'm too big for that sort of mothering. But I'll miss her when we've gone. I can feel a pit of loneliness growing deep inside me, but I blink back my tears and stand up straight. I have to be strong like Mum because I've got to take Mum's place in our new home. And if I get upset now, so will Elsie and I don't want my little sister to travel the whole way in wet knickers.

In that example, I'm still inside Daisy's head so I can see what she sees and know what she knows. But this time I'm pretending I really am Daisy so I'm writing in the first person, referring to her as *I* and talking about *my nose* and *our new home*. If I'd written this in the past tense, it would have been almost exactly the same as the previous third person example, except for the changes of pronoun (I held tight, I ducked my head, etc.). But I switched to the present tense because that's a popular choice with first person viewpoint, especially in young adult novels. Using the present tense has the advantage of allowing the viewpoint character to be surprised by events in a way that is hard to achieve when they are recounting events that have already happened to them.

As you can see, the scene has more immediacy when it's written in third person close or first person – from the inside looking out. That helps you identify more strongly with Daisy and care about what's happening to her. We always want to make our readers care, so these two viewpoints are the best choices for most novels.

Viewpoint problems

There are two snags with both first person and third person close.

- You can't tell the reader anything that happens while the viewpoint character isn't there.

- You can't reveal what any other character is thinking, although you can mention behaviour that hints at what's going through their minds.

If you want to continue the story of the evacuees through Daisy Spike's eyes, you have to travel on the train with her. You can't show what happens when Mum goes home or reveal what Mum was thinking about the lack of photographs. If Daisy's London home is destroyed in a bombing raid, the reader won't know about it until Daisy does.

Similarly, if you're writing a thriller in the third person and an attacker is stalking your viewpoint character on a dark night, you can only tell the reader about him if your character knows he's there too. If she doesn't, the eventual attack will be a total surprise for the readers as well as the victim.

But some stories work better if the reader knows more than the main character. Maybe you want to build tension by letting your reader see a danger ahead that your hero doesn't know is there or by letting your heroine believe her lover is dead while the readers know that he's not. The only way to do this is to switch to a different character's viewpoint or to use author view for some scenes.

Using multiple viewpoints

Multi-viewpoint story telling can work well. You can write each viewpoint in the third person, mix first person for one character with third person for others or even use first person for more than one character. But changing viewpoint too often can confuse your readers and make it harder for them to care about what's happening. To avoid these problems, it's best to minimize the number of characters whose eyes you look through and not switch between them too often.

Wherever possible, only change viewpoint when there is a natural break in the story. Changing mid-conversation, mid-fight or mid-scene can muddle your readers and make them step back from the storyline while they sort out who is doing what. If you find yourself switching viewpoint in the middle of the action, look carefully at what's happening in the plot and try to come up with an alternative way of handling the scene that doesn't require it. But if you decide there really is no alternative, help your readers by making it as clear as possible that the viewpoint has changed.

Viewpoint issues in children's books

Using more than one viewpoint makes your readers work harder because they have to keep track of who is telling the story at any given point in time. This can cause problems for children who have only just learned to read. They are already putting so much effort into deciphering the words that it's easy for them to lose track of what's happening. That's why I always stick to one viewpoint when I'm writing for that group.

However, multiple viewpoints can work very successfully with older children. In *Harry Potter and the Philosopher's Stone*, J K Rowling uses author's view (omniscient viewpoint) for much of chapter one and the start of chapter two, but she switches to Harry's viewpoint as soon as he wakes up in the cupboard under the stairs. She sticks to this for most of the rest of the book, but there are scenes from other points of view when the reader needs to know more than Harry. And, judging by the success of the book, that works well for her readers.

How viewpoint affects plotting

It's important to be aware of the viewpoint issue while you are plotting because which one you choose will determine which events you can show and which will have to be reported.

Let's look again at the first few steps in the plot for *Future Proof.*

1. Seb is demolishing an empty house when he finds an old diary hidden under the floorboards. It's in French so he can't read it.

2. Seb starts to take it to his boss but hesitates. Money is tight and this might be valuable to a collector. But it's hard to know how much it's worth without knowing what it says.

3. He takes the diary to Jane and asks her to translate it.

4. Jane won't do it. The study of history is strictly controlled and she'll get into trouble if she works on an unauthorized artefact.

5. Seb persuades her to change her mind by tempting her to tackle something new instead of the dry, approved texts she usually has to translate. Jane agrees reluctantly, worried she'll be caught and get into trouble.

6. Jane starts to translate the diary and quickly discovers that it contains a different version of history from the one she's always been told was true.

At the moment, steps 1 and 2 have to be from Seb's point of view because Jane isn't there. 3, 4 and 5 could be written from either viewpoint and step 6 might work best if it was in Jane's. So which viewpoint should I use: Jane's or Seb's or both (switching from scene to scene as seems appropriate)?

All three options are equally valid, but each will make me tell the story in a different way. If I use Jane's viewpoint, I won't be able to show Seb finding the diary. Readers won't know of its existence until Seb shows it to her, and they will only discover why he has it when he explains that to her. That's going to give me a lot of telling to do right at the beginning of the story which may make it harder to capture the readers' attention.

If I use Seb's viewpoint, readers will see him find the book, share his thoughts about what to do with it and see his approach to Jane for help through his eyes. However, they won't be able to hear her internal arguments about whether to help him or not so I'll have to either make her say them aloud or let her body language show her reluctance. They also won't be able to share her thoughts as she translates the diary.

There are downsides to both options so I'm going to try using both viewpoints, starting in Seb's and switching to Jane's later at about the time she receives the diary. If I want to, I can then stay in Jane's viewpoint for the rest of the book but it will probably be useful to use Seb's viewpoint in other places too, especially if my two main characters become separated.

23

Choosing where to start

Have you ever read a novel that takes ages to get going? I know I have. Instead of diving into the action, the author spends ages setting the scene and introducing the main character. There's lots of description but very little actually happening so boredom starts to set in, which runs the risk of readers shutting the book for good. Of course, as a writer you may want to start slowly so that you can explore your characters and get to know them better. If so, feel free to write the opening, but don't assume that your readers need to read it. Instead, put it with your plot development notes and start the actual book at the point when the story starts.

Usually that point is at or just before the moment when your main character discovers the problem they are going to have to solve. In *The Bear Santa Claus Forgot* (which we looked at earlier), the book starts just before the bear falls out of the sack. It doesn't waffle on about how he was made, how he was put in the sack or how Santa circled the globe delivering all the other presents because none of those things are relevant to the story.

Even if you decide not to start with the problem itself, try to begin your book with some action that will capture the reader's attention and pull them into the story. But don't worry if you can't immediately see how you're going to do that. One of the delights of step outlining is that you can get on with creating the rest of the plot even though you haven't decided on the opening scene. Sometimes I don't manage to sort out where I'm going to start a story until I'm nearly ready to begin writing it.

What about prologues?

There are two main types of prologue. The first shows an important event from the past that will impact on the story or gives vital background information to help us understand how a character behaves. For example, a fantasy prologue might show the origins of a vital prophecy while a psychological thriller might start with a prologue showing the childhood trauma that destroyed the murderer's sanity.

The second type shows a scene from later in the book or even further in the future. It's a teaser designed to catch readers' attention and make them read on to discover why that scene happened. But it's a risky technique because it can also act as a spoiler that takes away the suspense of not knowing what's going to happen.

The problem with both types of prologue is summed up in the words of a boy I once watched open a new book. "Oh, it's got a prologue," he said, with obvious disappointment. "I never bother to read those." I sympathize with him. I've never been much of a prologue fan myself, and I know he's not the only one who doesn't read them.

So, if you're tempted to include a prologue in your novel, ask yourself if your readers will understand the story if they skip it? If they will, do you need the prologue at all? If they won't, can you make your prologue into chapter one to make sure everyone reads it? Alternatively, can you provide the vital information it contains in some other way? With careful thought and skilful writing, you can probably do away with the need for a prologue altogether. Only include one if there's no alternative.

For example, in *Harry Potter and the Philosopher's Stone*, chapter one describes the important events that took place when Harry was a baby. These happened long before the rest of the book takes place, so J K Rowling could have put them in a prologue. But they work fine as a first chapter, and putting them there makes sure that everyone reads them, even those who hate prologues.

Putting theory into practice

As I've decided to begin *Future Proof* in Seb's viewpoint, I can start the story with the event that's going to change his life – finding the diary. I can emphasise the potential danger by showing his boss warning him that anything found has to be handed in, and then let the readers share the thoughts that result in him deciding to keep the book.

The start of the story for Jane is when Seb gives her the diary so, if I was writing in her viewpoint, I'd need that moment close to the beginning of the book. But I don't think it would work to have that as the opening scene. It would be better to have another scene first that introduces Jane and hints at the world in which she lives. Readers will find it easier to understand her unwillingness to get involved initially if they already have some indication of the way history is controlled and the dangers the diary might bring.

A scene in the museum would be good. How about a school visit? That would provide some useful action, introduce Jane and, if she talks to the children, she could tell them some history that readers would easily recognize as wrong. If Seb comes with the class as a voluntary helper, he'll meet Jane and either take that opportunity to show her the book or return later to do it.

The more I think about it, the more I like the school visit idea. I'm definitely going to use it, even though I'm going to start the story in Seb's viewpoint, as it will be a great way to introduce Jane and provide more information on the world they live in.

In the process of working all that out, I've also decided that Seb isn't going to find a diary. He's going to find a time capsule – the sort that people love hiding in buildings. It's a tin box containing a couple of objects that he will hand in and a notebook that he decides to keep. (He might keep something else too, but I'm not sure yet.) So I've changed my mind yet again without having to do any rewriting. Three cheers for step outlining.

Here's my latest version.

1. A wrecking ball crashes into an empty house, reducing it to rubble.

2. A supervisor (maybe in uniform) orders Seb and some other labourers to go in and clear up the mess. He warns them that if they find anything old, they must hand it in at once. The way he behaves suggests that this is a rule that shouldn't be broken.

3. Seb is stacking bricks when he finds a tin box hidden in the base of a wall. He checks no one is looking and opens it. Inside are several photographs, including one in an ornate frame, a few other things and a notebook.

4. Seb hesitates. The risk is great but money is tight and the photo frame might fetch a good price on the black market. He slips it into his pocket and adds the notebook as an afterthought because he's curious about it. Then he reports the box and what's left inside.

5. After his morning's work, he slips into an alleyway and looks at the notebook. But he can't read it – it's in a language he doesn't know or maybe in code.

6. He goes to the local primary school were he has volunteered to spend the afternoon helping with a class visit to the museum.

7. The school visit is hectic. Jane tries to explain the exhibits and is bombarded with questions. Seb is impressed by her

and her obvious skills. (I need to work in something here to help him decide he can trust her.)

8. After the visit is over, Seb returns and talks to Jane. He shows her the notebook, pretending it's a modern one from a friend, and asks her to decipher it. But Jane isn't fooled. She can tell that the paper is very old. She strokes it lovingly – she rarely gets to handle anything that's really from the past – the exhibits at the museum are mainly replicas.

9. Jane doesn't want to get involved because she'd get into trouble if she was caught. The study of history is strictly controlled and she's forbidden to work on unauthorized artefacts.

10. Seb persuades her to change her mind by telling her about the box. If someone went to so much trouble to hide the notebook, it deserves to be read and it might be really important. Surely she's tempted?

11. Jane starts to translate the book and discovers that it reveals that history has been changed. It tells of a different past from the one she and everyone she knows have always been told was true. The elite who rule the world are ruthless. They took power by force, but keep the ordinary population in ignorance and poverty, suppressing all knowledge of alternative governments and democracy.

12. Jane comes under suspicion because she accidentally reveals that she knows more than she's supposed to.

13. She escapes and turns to Seb for help. He got her into this so he needs to get her out of danger. They run.

14. They decide to try to locate a rebel group.

15. Something happens.

16. Something else happens.

17. They find the rebels they've been searching for.

18. The rebels turn out differently from how they'd expected.

19. Seb and Jane decide to leave and find a better way to overthrow the elite.

20. A lot more happens.

21. The elite are overthrown.

The beginning is now much more detailed, but the end is still vague and the middle is virtually non-existent. I need to do more brainstorming and planning to work out the details.

24

Making every step count

One of the most useful pieces of writing advice I was ever given is "Everything you write must either build character, add humour or move the story forward." Sadly I can't remember where I first heard this, but it's stayed with me always and has hugely improved the quality of my writing. However, several writing friends have found it confusing so I'm going to adapt it slightly to make it more relevant to plotting. Here is my version:

Every step in your plot should perform at least one of these functions:

- **Give your reader useful information about a character or the setting.**

- **Move the story forward**

As an example, let's imagine that I've put a step in the outline for *Future Proof* that says "Jane makes a cup of tea." When I write the book, that could become something like this:

> *Jane reached up into the cupboard and selected a pink mug decorated with a fluffy kitten. She placed the mug on the work surface, put in a teabag and poured on boiling water. She waited until the water had turned*

a murky brown. Then she lifted out the bag and poured in the milk.

That step fails on both counts: it doesn't tell us anything important about Jane or the world she lives in and it doesn't move the story forward. So it's not plotting – it's padding.

A simple way to deal with this is to cut that step out of the plot completely. And you can do the same with all the other mundane parts of life like washing, brushing teeth, making polite conversation and taking uneventful journeys. Skipping over them will tighten your storytelling and let your readers concentrate on the events that are really important.

However, those same mundane activities can sometimes provide a useful backdrop for revealing important information about your characters and how they feel. For example, here is a tea-making scene that matters.

Jane's hands shook as she poured boiling water onto a tiny portion of her few precious tea leaves. She must have been crazy to agree to do something so dangerous. As soon as she could, she'd give the notebook back to Seb and pretend none of this had ever happened.

With her mind made up, she strained the weak tea into her favourite mug and carried it into the living room. But she couldn't stop thinking about the notebook. Surely it wouldn't hurt to look at it again – just once. She put down the mug, pulled the book out of her pocket and ran her fingers gently over its pages. Paper! Real paper with words no one had seen for years and years. How could she say "no" to a chance like this? She curled up in a battered armchair and started to read.

This version develops Jane's character by showing her doubts, and it also tells us a little about the world she lives in by mentioning the shortage of tea. Most importantly, it contains the pivotal moment where Jane puts her doubts aside and commits to reading the notebook – an important step in the plot and one that definitely moves the story forward.

All I need to write in the step outline is "Jane worries about getting into danger but starts to read the notebook anyway." I don't need to mention the tea as I can work out the exact detail of the step at the writing stage. But there is nothing wrong with mentioning it if that scene is already clear in my mind.

What about description?

The two functions rule doesn't rule out passages of description because they can reveal vital information about a character or setting. But it's often more interesting for the reader if you work the description into the story in a way that justifies mentioning it. For example, suppose you want to include a description of a beautiful sunset. You could make this relevant to the plot by showing a character watching the sun go down, making the setting sun shine in someone's eyes at a crucial moment or letting the failing light make it difficult for your characters to continue their search for clues.

Show, don't tell

One of the most common pieces of advice given to writers is *show, don't tell*. This often causes confusion, especially with beginners. After all, storytelling is what authors do so how can telling be wrong? Worse still, following this advice too rigidly can result in boring stories because showing isn't always the best option.

Going back to the tea-making scene we looked at earlier, both ways I have written it are *showing* because we can see exactly what happened. But if I wrote something like *Jane made a cup of tea*, I would be *telling*. In the first example where nothing happens other than tea-making, telling would be a better option as it would avoid boring the readers. In the second example, just saying *Jane made a cup of tea* would lose much of the emotional impact of the scene.

On the whole, the decision on when to show or tell comes in at the writing stage, but it can affect how you create your story so it's worth bearing in mind while you plot. Showing is usually best for important steps, but telling can be the right choice for minor steps and for linking steps together.

25

Subplots and story strands

A good way to stop your book being too predictable is to add some subplots. They will also help you pace the story and keep the tension rising. Unfortunately, the name "subplots" wrongly suggests they are somehow inferior or substandard. It also gives the impression that they are something separate from the main plot – a second story running under the first one and completely disconnected from it.

I sometimes find subplots like that in novels I read – usually the ones that aren't very good. The authors have realized that there's not enough going on in their book so they have stuck in a completely irrelevant subplot about a lost cat or a child's birthday that gets in the way of the main story and slows up the action.

I prefer to think of story strands rather than subplots as that better explains how they work. The main storyline is your central strand carrying the reader forward towards the final conclusion of the book. Other story strands (or subplots) intertwine with the main one, building it up from a single strand into a fascinating, deeply textured plot that will hold your readers' interest. If you've ever plaited hair, you'll know that different strands become the top one as you work and writing an interwoven plot is just like that. Although you have the main storyline running through the whole novel, other story strands will be more important at various stages of the book and some of the twists and turns in the plot come when you move from one strand to another or when two strands collide.

The story strands work together to carry the reader towards the end of the book and some, but not necessarily all, will be resolved at or around the same time as the resolution of the main storyline. Others will be resolved during the progress of the story, but this needs to be done with care or, going back to our hair analogy, you'll end up with an untidy plait with lots of straggly bits sticking out the sides.

One big advantage in thinking about story strands rather than subplots is that you don't have to worry whether a strand is big enough to count as a subplot in its own right or is really part of the main story. It won't make any difference to your writing either way so you can leave that question for people who try to analyse your book after it's finished. All you need to know is that the strand is there so you can use it to the best possible effect. (Incidentally, the better your book is plotted, the harder it is for analysts to tease apart the various strands of the story.)

How many strands does a book need?

Short stories and children's picture books work well with just a single storyline. (In writing jargon, they have a basic linear plot.) However, longer novels are more interesting if they have more than one strand and the longer the book, the more strands you can include. My Pony-Mad Princess books are around 7000 words long and usually have two strands. Usually one is about the ponies and the other is about the royal world, and I always aim to end both strands in the final chapter. For example, the strands in *Princess Ellie's Secret* are:

A. Ellie trying to stop her first pony being sold.

B. The problems caused by grumpy Great Aunt Edwina coming to stay at the palace.

(Warning: Spoilers ahead for pony-mad children.)

The plot starts with strand A. Ellie has outgrown her Shetland pony, Shadow, and is horrified when the King declares he must be sold because he has no work to do. She decides that she could drive him instead of riding him so secretly starts training him to pull a carriage. Then, just as everything seems to be going well, the plot twists with the introduction of strand B. Great Aunt Edwina has invited herself to stay at the palace and Ellie's parents give her the task of entertaining the grumpy old lady. This means Ellie can't spend any time at the stables.

After a frustrating time with her great aunt, Ellie manages to escape for a while to take Shadow for his first drive (back to strand A). Everything is going well until they turn a corner and come face to face with Great Aunt Edwina, who has gone out for a walk (strands A and B collide and join together). To Ellie's surprise, Great Aunt Edwina is delighted. She always liked driving when she was a girl and insists that Ellie moves over so she can take the reins. The King is so pleased to find something that makes his difficult aunt happy that he agrees to keep Shadow so she can drive him (strands A and B end together).

Mirrored strands

In the plot I've just described, the strand about the outgrown pony is the main storyline while the strand about Great Aunt Edwina is a secondary strand that's designed to complicate the plot. But you can also achieve a strong plot by making two strands of your story complement or mirror each other.

In my young adult novel, *There Must Be Horses*, one story strand is about the way Sasha's troubled background has left her unable to trust other people, and another strand is about a horse whose troubled background has made him unable to trust humans. As these mirrored strands weave together, the girl and the horse heal each other and solve each other's problems. There are plenty of other strands that make up the complete plot, but I am sure it is this mirroring that makes the conclusion of the book so emotionally satisfying for readers. (Most people cry happy tears when they are reading it, and I cried too when I was editing it.)

Unconnected strands

In another type of plot, the story strands are completely separate at first, and readers don't see the connection between them until later in the book. For instance, in a disaster story, you might introduce three or four completely separate characters in different situations and move between them, building up their individual story strands until some big event (like an earthquake or a war) brings them together. Similarly, in a thriller, you might create one story strand about a detective and another strand about a girl, both of which seem completely unconnected until the girl is murdered.

When you jump around between strands like this, experienced readers will assume that there will eventually be a link between them so they will be looking for it. You can play along with this by hinting at possibilities and building up some tension about when the link will be revealed.

Although this approach can work well, it can be hard to hold your readers' attention if you jump between characters so much that they are not sure which one they should be caring about. You can make life easier for them by introducing one character first and only introducing the others when their strands meet. So, in the thriller, you could concentrate on the girl until she's murdered and then introduce the detective's story strand, Or, alternatively, you could concentrate on the detective until the murder and then let him piece together the girl's story as he investigates the crime. In *Future Proof*, I'm going to introduce Seb first and only introduce Jane when Seb's story strand brings him into contact with her.

Weaving strands together

If your story has two or more main strands, it's sometimes difficult to decide how to weave them together. When I'm faced with this problem, I find it helpful to write a step outline for each strand of the story, putting each step on a separate sticky note and using different colours for each strand. Then I experiment with different ways to join those steps into one coherent plot by moving the pieces of paper around. The result is a single, multicoloured line of sticky notes – much like the plait I talked about earlier.

26

Creating story strands

All good stories involve at least one character with a problem, and the same is true of story strands. Your existing characters and their backstories can usually feature in more than just the main storyline. One obvious, but often useful additional strand is a romance between two of them, although a love triangle has even more potential because jealousy is such a powerful emotion.

Alternatively, you can create a new strand about an existing character by introducing a new fact about them that will affect the way they behave. Maybe they feel responsible for their sister's death in a childhood accident and therefore annoy the other characters by being overprotective. Or perhaps they are gay and struggle with feelings of attraction that they don't know whether to show or not. It's up to you when you reveal this secret to the reader. If you do it early on, they can share the character's struggle to resolve the issue. If you do it later, you'll keep them guessing about behaviour they can't understand which may intrigue them enough to keep reading.

Another useful way to add a new story strand is to add a new character – maybe a stranger comes to town, a new player joins the team or someone is spotted spying on your main character. They will bring their own story strand with them, and their arrival will upset the relationships between your characters which may, in turn, create new strands or help develop existing ones.

Making strands relevant

It's important that each strand you add must connect in some way to the main one, even if that connection isn't obvious at first. That happens naturally if the strand involves the same characters, but you need to plan carefully to make it happen when you introduce someone new.

Suppose you want to introduce a minor storyline about Mrs Morris and her lost puppy that is currently free-standing with no connection to your main characters or the events that surround them. Left like that, your readers will find the story an irritating diversion from the main plot, so it's best to either leave it out or change the story strand so it can be easily woven into the story. Here are some ways we could do that in *Future Proof*.

- Let Mrs Morris be the proprietor of a hotel where Seb and Jane stop to rest during their search for the rebels. They could be drawn into the search for the puppy and, as a result, find something important to the main storyline or miss a vital clue because they were distracted.

- Let Seb and Jane discover the lost puppy has been kidnapped by the rebels and slaughtered as a terrible warning of what might happen to anyone who betrays the rebellion. So the fate of the puppy is a sign that the rebels may be as much of a problem as the aliens.

- Let Mrs Morris be Jane's boss at the museum. Her preoccupation with the lost puppy makes her forget to lock her office when she goes out which gives Jane the opportunity to search her computer for vital information.

- Let Mrs Morris not really have a puppy. She only thinks she's lost one because her mind has been damaged by the aliens. This reveals a new danger for Seb and Jane as they may share her fate if they are captured.

Each of these options will move the story in a new direction, and our readers will find some of them more satisfying than others. (It's always best to avoid slaughtering puppies when you're writing for children.) The same is true when you try to deal with a disconnected story strand in your own novel. Do some brainstorming to see if you can weave it into the plot successfully. But, if you fail to think of a solution, be prepared to ditch that story strand completely as I am going to do with Mrs Morris and her puppy. Hopefully you'll be able to use it eventually in a different book.

Story strand creation in action

Future Proof is definitely in need of some extra story strands. An obvious one is the developing relationship between Seb and Jane which may or may not turn into a romance. (I don't know yet, and I'm planning to keep my readers guessing for quite a while.) To introduce some conflict and possible jealousy, I think I'll eventually introduce Gareth, another rebel who joins up with them as they search for a way to overcome their alien rulers.

I also want to introduce a character who is a rebel alien, unhappy with what his race are doing and willing to help the rebels. He offers lots of story potential, especially if he hides his true identity at first. He might turn out to be an alien spy. He might sacrifice himself to save the others. He might fall in love with Jane which would have all sorts of implications. Of course, I've already got Gareth in that last role, and it's not a good idea to have too many similar characters. So maybe I should combine the two and make Gareth the secret alien.

When I created Seb, I made him someone who lives on the edges of the law – a situation that offers opportunities for story strands based on his earlier transgressions. Maybe there's a gang leader who is after him for some reason, or there are other criminals he could call on to help him.

Jane, on the other hand, currently has a more normal background but, to add another strand to her story, I could add a complication. Suppose her love of history comes from her father who is now so old and sick that she lives with him to make sure he is looked after. That's going to make it harder for her to leave in search of the rebels which is great because you never want to make life easy for your main character.

Let's give Dad his own strand too. Although he is old and frail, his brain is as alert as ever. He has always been open minded to new ideas so he believes that what Jane has discovered about the aliens is true and wants to help her. When she and Seb have to flee for their lives, Dad could come to their rescue – sacrificing what's left of his own life to help them escape. That's a story strand packed with conflict and emotion. I'm definitely going to use it.

Staying flexible

The main storyline of your book is the one you would talk about if you were asked to describe your book in one sentence. This is sometimes called the elevator pitch, because it's what you might say if you got in a lift with a top publisher or agent and had to sell your book to them between floors.

As you work on your plot, you may find that one of your new story strands resonates with you and starts to take over from that original idea. If that happens, follow your instincts. If you're sure that you can make the new strand work better than your original main storyline, swap them over. You are only at the plotting stage so it's easy to do and there's no major rewriting involved, even if you eventually decide to swap them back.

27

Conflict, dilemmas and problems

The word *conflict* turns up in most books about plotting because it's so important in making stories work. However, it's one of the concepts I found most confusing when I was learning how to be a writer, and I am sure I am not alone in this.

The problem is that most of us think of conflict purely as physical fights and wars. But it occurs in many other forms too: explorers battle against the forces of nature, detectives struggle to outwit cunning criminals and doctors fight to save lives. All these situations can form the basis of a good story, but a story isn't just a string of events. It's an account of how those events affect the characters.

That's why the conflicts that are often most powerful in storytelling are the ones that go on inside your characters' heads while they struggle to decide what to do or force themselves to overcome their fears. These are often called internal conflicts but, because conflict is such a confusing word, let's call them dilemmas. In *Future Proof*, Seb faces a dilemma when he has to decide whether to keep the diary or hand it in to the authorities while Jane faces one when he asks her to break the law by translating the diary in secret.

The problem/dilemma connection

A dilemma doesn't happen in isolation. It's always closely tied to a problem. Let's leave *Future Proof* for a while, and imagine a character called Ben who is caught up in a volcanic eruption. He's managed to escape to his car and is about to drive away to safety.

Problem

As Ben reaches out to start the ignition, he hears a child crying for help in a house that's about to be engulfed by the approaching lava.

Dilemma

Should he drive away and leave the child to certain death, or risk his own life by trying to save her?

Result

The action he decides to take will move the story onto a new track. It will also reveal a great deal about Ben. If he goes back, he is obviously brave (and may end up dead). If he doesn't, is he a coward or is he totally unfeeling? Will leaving the child to die scar him for life and affect how he handles other crises in the future?

That was a life-and-death situation with all the tension it brings with it. Let's look at a non-fatal example where what's at stake is success. Anne is an athlete who is desperate to leave her small town behind. She's been offered a place on the national team provided her relay team win their next race. But the competition is fierce.

Problem

One of her team members admits she's been taking performance-enhancing drugs, and she offers some to Anne.

Dilemma

What should Anne do? Should she take the drugs and improve her chance of winning, refuse them and report her team member to the authorities or refuse the drugs and keep quiet so she can benefit from the other team member taking them?

Result

Her decision will determine where the story goes next and reveal crucial details about Anne's character.

Whatever the situation, the problem and the dilemma (or conflict) are tied so strongly together that it's virtually impossible to have one without the other. The problem comes first, the dilemma happens as your character struggles to cope with it and that in turn results in an action which will move the story forward. Unless you've reached the end of your book, that action will almost certainly lead on to another problem that will result in another problem/dilemma/action sequence. And a string of problem/dilemma/action sequences gives you a story.

To show you how that can happen, let's imagine a character called David who is being chased through a forest by a pack of hungry wolves. Although there are plenty of trees, he can't climb them because their branches are too high. Suddenly he spots one with a conveniently low branch so he grabs hold of it, hoping to climb to safety.

Problem

That convenient low branch snaps off in his hand. There's no way he can climb the tree now, and the wolves are closing in.

Dilemma

Should he run again or try to fight?

Action

He turns to face the wolves with his back to the tree. He shouts at the wolves and waves the broken branch at them.

Problem:

The wolves hesitate at first, then creep forward growling menacingly. (*Do wolves growl – I need to check on that.*)

Dilemma

This isn't going to work. And they are too close now to run from. What else can he do?

Action

He pulls off his bandana, wraps it round the end of the branch and sets fire to it with a lighter he conveniently has in his pocket. (*Need to mention this earlier so it doesn't look too contrived.*) He waves the burning branch at the wolves, and they draw back.

Problem

As he waves the branch, it touches the dry leaves covering the forest floor and they start to burn. Flames leap up, fanned by the strong breeze. (*something else to mention earlier*). The wolves run off in fear but the fire remains, spreading rapidly and racing towards David.

Dilemma

Running is the obvious action – the question is where? Water is the only thing that can save him now.

Action

He races downhill, hoping to find a stream.

So that sequence has changed the story from one about attacking wolves to one about a deadly forest fire. It has shown David to be resourceful and determined and given him a possible escape route, although that probably won't go smoothly.

As you can see, once you've found the problem, the dilemma and the action follow naturally. So when I'm plotting, I spend a lot of my time creating problems for my characters. I often make these build on the one before, as I did with David and the wolves, but occasionally I throw in one that's completely unexpected to twist the story in a new direction.

Types of problem

Many problems are physical – locked doors are popular and so are cliff edges, raging torrents and landslides. If you are writing a fantasy quest, you can choose from an even wider selection, including man-eating spiders, fire-breathing dragons and forests of moving trees designed to lure travellers to their doom. Any danger can work provided it fits into your story and strikes fear into the hearts of your readers as well as your characters.

Weather is a good provider of physical problems, which is one reason why the final scenes in a drama often happen during a storm. Strong winds can block roads with fallen trees, whip calm seas into mountainous waves and make walking outside a dangerous activity. Rain can cause floods, wash away vital footprints and chill travellers to the bone, while snow blankets the footprints that haven't been washed away, makes places look completely different and puts lives at risk when it tumbles down mountainsides in devastating avalanches.

But not all problems are physical. Many of the best ones come from the characters in your story and from the way they interact with each other and with the world. Face them with difficult decisions, give them past experiences that affect the way they react to the present, reveal secrets when they are sure to have maximum impact and never, ever let the course of true love run smooth. That way you'll end up with a story packed with various types of conflict, even if you're still not sure what the word actually means.

The trouble with phones

Once upon a time, it was easy to put your characters in a tricky situation packed with problems. They could get lost, wandering for hours in forests or deserts with no idea where they were. They could find themselves in danger but unable to call for help. They could be in desperate need of information but not know where to find it.

Then someone invented the mobile phone (or cell phone for those of you in the USA). Thanks to that handy gadget clutched in their hands, your characters can easily find vital facts, contact other people and, worst of all, call for help. And they are very rarely lost. As soon as they find themselves in unfamiliar territory, they can just turn to their phone and call up Google Maps. They'll not only discover exactly where they are – they'll also get directions on how to find their way home and probably be able to call a taxi to pick them up.

One way to avoid the phone issue is to set your story back in time before they were invented or move it forward to a time when the wretched things are banned. But if you're definitely writing about the present day, you'll need to make sure that your main character doesn't have a phone with them at times when having one would wreck the story. Luckily the fragility of phones means that they can be rendered useless by:

- Dropping them on something hard.

- Treading on them.

- Running them over with a car.

- Dropping them into water.

- Setting them on fire.

Failing any of those disasters, phones can run out of battery, which is very likely when a character is on the run and unable to plug in a charger. They can also be out of signal range. This frequently happens in my living room so it seems reasonable to believe that it would happen on a mountainside or deep in a forest.

Luckily the bad guys are as aware of phone problems as we are so the first thing they are likely to do when they capture someone is to take away their phone. If you think your character will need it later in the story, make your villains put it somewhere safe: it can then be found at a convenient moment. Otherwise they can dramatically destroy it in front of your character's eyes to make their situation even worse.

Of course, phones don't always get in the way in a story. They can also provide problems for your characters in the form of anonymous messages or incriminating photographs, and they can allow the bad guys to pinpoint their position. There are even rumours that security services can turn on a phone's microphone from a distance to use as a bugging device – a process that could add another complication to your story.

Putting theory into practice

Let's go back to *Future Proof* to see how we can add problems and dilemmas for Seb and Jane to keep the story running and readers turning the pages. Phones (or their future equivalent) aren't an issue as I've decided ordinary people aren't allowed to use them. But disagreement is always a good cause of problems. That's why I'm going to make Seb want to take the diary to the rebels, but Jane not be quite so sure. She's not convinced that the situation is as bad as it says. Surely she'd know if there really were aliens running the world? Anyway she's got responsibilities looking after her dad. She can't just leave him. There must be another solution: someone in authority who can help them get the information into the right hands.

She turns to her boss at the museum for advice. But he betrays them to the police, who try to arrest them. Seb and Jane escape just in time, but Jane is still unwilling to leave her dad because he is sick and dependent on her. She can't leave him behind so she insists on going home to collect him.

To her surprise, Dad believes what the diary says. But he refuses to go with her, because he'll slow her down. Jane argues, unable to accept they have to separate. Then the police arrive, and there is no more time for goodbyes.

Dad pushes her out the back door, promising to slow the police as long as he can and point them in the wrong direction. Seb and Jane run away while the police arrive, interrogate Dad and shoot him. The realization that her dad has sacrificed himself to save her and the diary gives Jane the reason she finally needs to commit herself to search for the rebels with Seb.

That last scene is going to take some thought. Is Jane going to watch the police arrive or am I going to switch viewpoints to let readers see what happens to Dad while she's not there? However, I don't have to decide on all those details while I'm plotting. I can sort out them out when I'm doing the actual writing.

In that section, one problem led naturally to another. Now let's put in one that adds an unexpected twist to the plot. It's going to happen much later in the story, and it might make a good end point for book one if I do decide to write a trilogy.

Seb and Jane have met Gareth, fellow opponent of the elite who joins their search for the rebel headquarters. A strong love triangle has developed, and Jane has been in a quandary for some time, trying to resolve her growing feelings for Seb with her strong attraction to Gareth. Finally she and Gareth are alone together, and they move towards each other. With a thumping heart, she lifts her face to kiss him but as she does so, she sees a flash of silver in his eyes and realizes he is an alien.

This neatly turns the story in a new direction and faces Jane with new questions and dilemmas. Is Gareth a traitor or a spy? Should she tell Seb? Should she kill Gareth? If he's a spy, can she turn him into a double agent? But in order for the scene to work, I'll have to go back in the plot to plant the fact that the diary says aliens have silver eyes but warns that they can hide this except at moments of great emotion. I can also plant a couple of clues to

Gareth's true identity that are subtle enough for readers to miss but obvious enough that when the big reveal comes, they say "of course" rather than "no way".

28

Pacing your book

If you are planning a car journey, the fastest route between your starting point and your destination is a straight, fast road. But that's likely to be so uninteresting that it causes the dreaded cry of "Are we nearly there yet?" from your passengers. They will be less bored if you take them on a route that provides ups and downs and changing scenery, but you need to keep an eye on where you're heading or you might get lost in a multitude of leafy lanes.

The same applies to plotting. If you choose the most obvious route to the end of your book, your readers will find it so easy to guess what's going to happen that they'll lose interest and stop reading. To hold their attention, you need to keep them guessing and keep them caring by adding unexpected twists and turns while always keeping moving towards that final satisfying end.

If you succeed, you should find that the closer your readers get to the end, the harder they find it to put the book down. When someone tells you they've read into the small hours to find out what happens, you know you've got everything right. In particular, you've paced the story well with rising tension to keep them reading and no boring bits to make them lose interest.

Tension can be tiring

Although we want the tension to rise throughout the book, it doesn't have to build at the same rate all the time. If it did, the shape of your story would look like this:

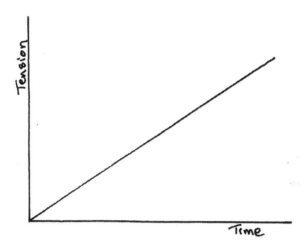

That can be exhausting for readers. It's better to intersperse tense sections with quieter moments to give readers time to relax slightly before the tension starts to build again.

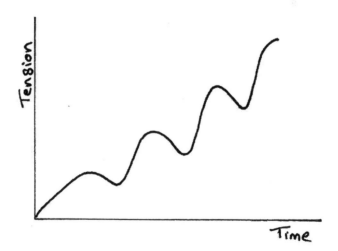

The exact shape will vary from book to book: yours will probably be different from my diagram. But the important things to remember are:

- Always have peaks and troughs.

- Make the final peak higher than any of the others to provide an exciting ending.

- Don't let any of the troughs go right back to zero. Always keep some tension running to hold the interest of the reader. If you don't, they may stop reading because they don't think anything else interesting is going to happen.

Keeping interest going

A good way to introduce a change in pace is to switch to a different story strand for a while. For example, the detective may leave the search for clues to deal with something at home, or the tumultuous romance may be interrupted by something happening at work. A change of viewpoint can also provide a way to change the pace without dropping the tension too much. For example, you could leave one character on a mountainside, dangling from a rope that's about to snap, and switch to the viewpoint of his friend who is waiting for him to come home, unaware that anything has gone wrong.

29

What's at stake?

The way your readers react to your story will depend on what's at stake. To show you how that works, let's imagine we're watching a wildlife documentary about foxes. There are three scenes, each of which follows a different fox as she hunts a rabbit.

Scene 1

This fox is plump, well fed and not hungry. She just fancies killing something for fun.

There's nothing at stake for the fox. She doesn't need to kill so I want the rabbit to get away.

Scene 2

This fox is thin and weak from lack of food. If she doesn't catch this rabbit, she may starve to death.

This time the fox's life is at stake so she has my sympathy. I understand her need to kill and, although I still feel sorry for the rabbit, I want her to catch it.

Scene 3

The fox is weak from hunger and has four starving cubs who will die if they don't eat soon.

Now it's not just her life at stake. The survival of four innocent babies depends on this hunt: I'm on the edge of my seat, urging her to succeed.

Increasing what's at stake for the fox has increased my sympathy for her. The more she stands to lose, the more I care about the outcome. And the same is true in stories – the more that will go wrong if your characters don't solve their problem, the more your readers will want them to succeed.

Life-or-death situations always create tension, but they don't fit neatly into every story. Luckily life isn't the only thing that can be lost: threats to happiness, freedom, love, family relationships, money, security and faith can all up the stakes enough to keep the tension in your story rising. In the children's story we looked at near the beginning of this book, it's Madeleine's happiness that's under threat. She'll be unhappy if her new bear isn't there when she wakes up in the morning, so the bear keeps trying to reach her and we keep urging him on.

You can have different things at stake in different strands of the story. In *Future Proof*, the central story has the ultimate danger – a threat to the future of mankind – while the dangers Seb and Jane meet in their search for the rebels will put both their lives at risk. But the story strand about the love triangle between Seb, Jane and Gareth has something else at risk: their individual happiness.

Increasing the stakes

One way to add rising tension to a story is to gradually increase what's at stake. Suppose a plot starts with a detective trying to solve an apparently straightforward murder. What's at stake at the beginning is justice for the victim. However, the detective gradually discovers that this murder is connected to corrupt politicians who are willing to do anything to stop him discovering what they are doing: a situation that puts first his job and then his life at risk.

When he finally discovers the politicians are trying to cover up safety problems at a nuclear power station, there is even more at stake – the safety of everyone who lives in the area – and that will lead to a really tense climax to the book.

30

Handling time

The way you handle time in your book will make a big difference to its pace. Over the years, I have learned that the shorter the time span the story covers, the easier it is to hold the readers' attention. As a result, I usually try to compress events into a few days rather than a few weeks, but sometimes that's just not possible. Then I have to use other techniques to stop the story dragging.

Time jumps

The fact that your story takes place over weeks, months or years doesn't mean you must include every detail of every day. It's better to concentrate on the main events of the plot and jump over the intervening time. Small time jumps are common in novels – in fact, it would be hard to find a story without at least one – and many books contain huge jumps, especially when the story covers a large part of a character's life.

You can often deal with small jumps in a few words such as "Four weeks later" or "The next four weeks flew past in a flurry of preparations." Longer gaps of months or years may need a bit more explanation. In *Jane Eyre*, Charlotte Brontë skips over eight years in five paragraphs at the start of chapter 10 to move the story from Jane's childhood experiences to her life as an adult.

Another way to deal with large time jumps is to divide your book into sections with each new section starting a new time period. The number of sections is entirely up to you. In *The Pillars of the Earth*, Ken Follett successfully uses six sections plus a prologue to cover 54 years.

But you don't need to work out all the details of how you are going to handle your time jumps at the plotting stage. You can just note that the time jump is there and decide how you are going to handle it when you are doing the actual writing.

Time travel

Books on time travel have time jumps for a different reason. To help your readers keep track of what's happening, you may want to put a time at the beginning of each chapter or section. Of course, that's not compulsory, and you may not want to do it if it removes an element of surprise from what comes next. On the other hand, if it suits your story, this approach can save you writing long passages of explanation and provide a useful reference point if your readers get confused.

Timelines

It's not just your readers who risk being confused about time. You can get in a muddle yourself, especially when you are trying to keep track of several story strands and characters at once. Then it's easy to make someone go out in the dark on a midsummer evening when it should still be light or pick an apple off a tree when it's supposed to be April.

A simple way to deal with this is to draw a timeline for your book, noting what happens when (day of the week, time). Depending on your story, you may also want to add the actual dates as well and write in any real historical events that are relevant. There are some useful websites that can tell you the day of the week for any date – past or future.

I sometimes draw several timelines underneath each other, one for each character or storyline, so I can check how the different steps line up and make sure that everyone is in the right place at the right time. For some stories, it's also useful to have another timeline showing events in the outside world.

In addition to or instead of a timeline, you can put the date and time on each step of your step outline or on each step where the time actually matters. This isn't essential but it can be useful with some stories, especially ones which include time travel or flashbacks.

Flashbacks

Flashbacks are a popular way to provide background information about characters or events. They let you use action and dialogue to dramatize scenes that happened in the past which is much more interesting for readers than just having one character relate what happened. However, they need to be used with caution or they may cause more trouble than they are worth.

The problem is that it's easy for readers to forget that what they are reading is a flashback. Then they get a shock when you return to the normal time in which your book is set, and that shock can jolt them out of the story completely. Interestingly, the same difficulty arises with dream sequences, so making your character dream the flashback doesn't avoid the issue.

Of course, you can avoid this problem completely by not using any flashbacks at all. They are not essential, and many books work well without them. But if you're sure that's what your plot needs, there are several ways to avoid causing confusion.

- Keep each flashback as short as possible so readers don't lose contact with the main story.

- Make the change to and from the flashback crystal clear. Sometimes it helps to use italics or indenting to make it obvious that this section is different from the main text.

- If you are sure you need a very long flashback, consider putting it in a separate section or chapter. You can put the date and place at the beginning of this to make the jump clearer and then put it again when you go back to normal time.

- Consider breaking a long flashback into two or more shorter ones with a return to normal time in between. The break doesn't have to be very long – a few lines of dialogue can sometimes be enough to remind your reader what's flashback and what isn't.

Time pressure

If your characters have all the time in the world to solve their main problem, there is no need for them to rush and the odd setback isn't a disaster. But if you think of some reason why they have to find the solution in a short period of time, you make their task much harder and the closer they get to the deadline, the more tense the situation will become. That's why there is always a timer ticking away the seconds while James Bond struggles to diffuse a bomb or Doctor Who tries to stop a spaceship autodestructing.

Time pressure doesn't just work in life-and-death situations. It is just as effective when a girl has two days to escape an arranged marriage, a detective has 24 hours to prove his innocence before he is suspended or the prince has three days to complete the task that will win him the hand of the princess he loves. But there needs to be something real at stake. The sort of artificial deadlines that crop up in reality TV shows don't work well in stories.

It's nearly always possible to add some time pressure to your plot if you think hard enough, and it can be a perfect way to build in some extra tension. For maximum effect, make life so difficult for your main characters that they run right up to the deadline and, if the tension starts to drop, make something happen to bring that deadline forward. Of course, you'll need to occasionally remind your readers of how much time is left (the literary equivalent of the ticking clock), but you can sort that out at the writing stage.

Future Proof offers plenty of possibilities for adding some time pressure. I could make Jane discover that the police are coming in ten minutes to arrest her for hiding the notebook, so she has to escape before they arrive. Or I could give Jane and Seb just three days to prevent a rebel attack that they know is doomed to fail. Or, if I make the aliens plan to destroy the human race in a week's time, our heroes would only have seven days to save mankind.

It's fine to use time pressure in more than one way in the same book provided you are careful to make the events they apply to sufficiently different from each other. So there's no reason why I can't use all of these ideas if I want to (although the last one will have to wait for the final book if I decide to write a trilogy).

31

When the plot goes wrong

I t's very difficult to get a story right first time. So the chances are very high that you'll hit a problem or get stuck at some point during the creation of your story. I know from experience that it's natural to feel downhearted when this happens, but try to resist the temptation to give up. Setbacks are a natural part of the writing process, so it's best to treat them as a challenge rather than a disaster. And sorting them out often makes your story better and more original than it was before.

The troubleshooting sections that follow this one are designed to help you work out what's wrong and decide how you are going to fix it. You'll probably also find it helpful to look back to relevant parts of the rest of this book. As with all aspects of plotting, don't assume that the first solution that comes into your head is the one you should use. Try to think of several different ways of dealing with the issue. Then look at their implications for the whole story before you decide which is going to work best.

Dealing with feedback

Sometimes you'll pick up a problem yourself during the initial plotting process or while you are doing the actual writing. However, you might not realize the story isn't working out as well as you'd hoped until you've finished the first draft and your test/beta readers or your editor point out some problems. (A fresh eye always picks up things you've missed. That's why beta readers and editors are so useful.)

It's tempting to argue with people who tell you the beginning is slow, they got bored in the middle or they got the characters muddled up. But there's no point. You can't change the way they feel, and there was no point in asking their opinion in the first place unless you are willing to listen to what they say. However, that doesn't mean you have to change absolutely everything they mention, and it definitely doesn't mean that you have to follow any suggestions they make to sort things out. Although any reader can spot a problem, it takes a writer to work out what's caused it and how best to sort it out. (The same is true of editors – editing and writing are different skills.)

Once you have all the feedback on your story, read your work through carefully with those comments in mind. Highlight everything you feel needs to be sorted out and do some troubleshooting to work out how you're going to do it. Then start rewriting. That's a very important stage in the creative process because it's the rewriting that makes a good book great.

32

Troubleshooting the beginning

When anyone starts to read your book, they will have lots of questions in their head. What's the story about? Where is it happening? When is it happening? Is it fantasy or real life? If it's fantasy, what kind of world is it? Who is the main character? What kind of person are they? What's their problem?

You don't need to answer all those questions immediately, but you do need to give them enough information to avoid confusion. And you need to do it in a way that holds their attention and draws them into the story. Here are some of the most common problems that arise and some suggestions on how to solve them.

The story takes too long to get going

- Start later.

- Check that all the early steps of your story are necessary. Leaving out the ones that aren't needed will speed up your story.

- Add a problem to an existing story strand or introduce a different strand to provide some early interest. You may not need to invent this strand from scratch – it can be one from later in the story that you decide to introduce earlier than you originally planned. Sometimes just a hint is enough to tweak the reader's curiosity.

- Dramatize a problem or event that's already there. At the beginning of a story, there's a big temptation to tell rather than show because you are concentrating on setting up the situation. But showing is what grabs the reader's attention and makes the characters come alive.

- Leave out any background information that isn't strictly necessary at the moment. You can put it in later.

The opening scene works well, but then the story slows right down

The most common reason for this is when you follow an exciting opening incident with a huge chunk of background information (sometimes called an infodump).

- Leave out any background information about the situation, setting or characters that isn't essential at this point in the story. You can add it later, if it's really needed.

- Tell the readers just enough to awaken their curiosity so they want to go on reading to find out more.

- Break the background information into small bits and drip-feed it to readers by giving it to them a little at a time while you continue to tell the story.

- Make the scene after the opening incident more interesting by giving a character a problem or dilemma, even if it's quite a small one.

Readers say they are confused by all the characters

- Introduce characters one at a time. Even if the story is about a group, you can concentrate on just one at first, then bring in the second, etc.

- Avoid naming any minor characters who crop up in the opening pages. Readers tend to assume that any character with a name needs to be remembered.

- Think whether you need so many characters. Combining two of them into one will cut the numbers, and it may produce a more rounded, interesting personality who adds extra potential to your story.

- Check the names of your characters and change any that are too similar to each other.

33

Troubleshooting the middle

The middle is the place you are most likely to run into problems. It's easy to get bogged down in detail or to be in such a rush to get to the end that you don't make the most of of the main events on the way. Here are some of the most common issues you are likely to face.

Readers lose interest

- Check that you are using the main events in your story as effectively as possible and making the most of their dramatic potential. These are the sections where you must show rather than tell.

- Add complications. Give your characters extra dilemmas and difficulties to overcome in existing story strands.

- Add new story strands to avoid the story being too linear.

- Take out any irrelevant padding as that's a sure cause of boredom.

- Increase what's at stake to make the story more compelling.

- Look at your main characters to see if you can spot ways to make your readers care more about them.

The story is repetitive

This can easily happen as your main characters keep trying unsuccessfully to solve their problem. It's also a common issue with quests and journeys which automatically have the "go somewhere – something happens – go somewhere else" format. To stop the story being repetitive, try some of these ideas.

- Consider cutting out some of the repetitive events. Remember the rule of three: try once and fail, try twice and fail, then succeed has a good rhythm. Even three fails followed by success works quite well. But more fails than that become repetitive unless you make them very different from each other.

- Vary the problems your characters face so they are not too similar or predictable.

- Vary the way your characters solve the problems to stop your story becoming a string of fights, arguments or running away.

- Use time jumps to vary the way you tell the story. You don't need a blow-by-blow account of every step of the journey so build up the most important steps and jump over the trivial bits (like washing, dressing and breakfasting) that tend to be very repetitive.

- Introduce another story strand to force your characters off course for a while. If you want, you can use the resulting delay to the main plotline to add some time pressure to keep the tension rising.

The story is too predictable

- Brainstorm fresh ideas, and opt for events that are less obvious.

- Introduce a fresh problem or character to move the story in a different direction.

- Reveal something unexpected about a character. Make a good one turn out to be bad or vice versa.

- Kill or injure someone. The more important they are to the plot, the more impact this will have. But beware of killing characters in children's books. It can have much more impact than you expected and really upset young readers and viewers.

- Introduce a physical problem to turn the story in an unexpected direction. An earthquake, storm, shipwreck, flood, car crash or train wreck are just a few of the possibilities. A bit of brainstorming will produce an even longer list.

34

Troubleshooting the end

It's easy to rush the end because you're excited about finishing your book. But it's important to take your time and get it right, because a good ending will make readers more likely to recommend your book to other people

The end is too predictable

- Do some brainstorming to come up with a different ending

- Complicate the existing ending by putting unexpected (but believable) problems in your characters' way.

- Make sure you have a black moment before the final success – a point where all seems lost. This could be your current ending – the one everyone is expecting – if you make it go horribly wrong.

Readers don't find the end believable

This most often happens when the final solution to your characters' problem rests on them having a skill your readers didn't know about or, in detective stories, a clue they didn't know about until the last page. It also happens when you make someone act completely out of character just to make the ending happen.

- Brainstorm alternative endings to see if you can think of a better one.

- Go back through the plot and work in steps that show that your character has the required skill or a believable reason for behaving in the way they do at the end.

- Make sure all necessary clues are in the story. If they are and your readers still don't find the end believable, you may need to emphasize the clues a little more.

Readers believe the ending but don't find it satisfying

The most common reason for this is that your main characters didn't solve the problem themselves.

- Change the end to one where the characters solve their own problem.

- If you need the police, cavalry or anyone else to come to the rescue, make sure they are there because your characters called them. Ideally make them come a little too late – just as your characters have won the fight, found the treasure or whatever.

- Make sure that the ending meets the expectations of your readers. They are unlikely to be pleased if the serial killer escapes or the romantic couple decide to split up forever. Even sad endings should offer some hope.

- If you are writing a series, make sure the ending provides a satisfying conclusion to some of the storylines, even though you leave some unresolved for later books.

35

Troubleshooting the length

Every story has its own length. Don't automatically assume you've done something wrong because yours has turned out shorter or longer than you expected. But if you want to change the length, try these ideas.

It's too short

- Check that you have dramatized the most important steps in the story. Telling is nearly always shorter than showing.

- Add a fresh problem, story strand or character (or maybe all three).

- DON'T pad out the story with irrelevant detail. That will not make your readers happy.

It's too long

- Take out irrelevant detail and description, including surplus adjectives and adverbs.

- Tell rather than show if the information is not important.

- Tighten dialogue, removing irrelevant chit-chat.

- Take out any steps or scenes that don't build character or move the story forward.

- Remove a minor story strand.

- Remove a minor character.

- Combine two characters into one.

- Combine two steps or scenes into one.

36

Choosing the title

I've left this section until last because that's where it comes in the plotting and writing process. While you are creating your book or novel, you can use any working title you like, however simple. But once you've finished, you'll need to decide on the real title before your book is published.

That decision is extremely important. The title is the first thing your potential readers will see, and how they react to it will help them decide whether to look at your book or not. So put as much thought into the title as you have done to every other aspect of your book. Have a brainstorming session and write a list of the ideas you like best.

Now search these on Amazon and Google to see if any of them have already been used. Although there is no copyright in titles, using one that's been used before may cause confusion and, if the other book is successful, it will stop your book showing up well on searches.

If you find other titles that are similar to your ideas, check to see if the books they belong to are similar to yours. Some title styles suggest particular genres and, if that genre doesn't fit your book, readers may be confused. This happened to me with *There Must Be Horses* which had *Sasha's Story* as its working title. Searching on Amazon showed that this type of title was particularly used for what the publishing industry calls misery memoirs: accounts of someone's miserable and often traumatic life. My book didn't fit that genre so I chose a new title, and this time I deliberately included the word *horse* to help attract horse lovers.

Once you have a shortlist of titles you think will work, try them out on as many potential readers as you can. Their reactions will help you make your final choice, and it may prevent you making a bad decision.

37

A final update on *Future Proof*

W e've nearly reached the end of this book and, as you've probably noticed, I haven't finished plotting *Future Proof*. That doesn't surprise me, because I only started creating the story to provide a way to show the plotting process in action. I never intended to actually write the novel. However, as so often happens during the plotting process, the characters and their stories have started to grow in my head and trigger questions.

- How will Seb and Jane find the rebels?

- What will happen when they reach the rebel base?

- Will Jane end up with Seb or Gareth?

- Will the aliens take revenge on Gareth for changing sides?

- Do the aliens run the whole world or just this part of it?

- Who hid the notebook?

I don't know the answers yet, but I want to find out. So one day, I hope to work out the rest of the plot. It's going to take me a long time, but if you ever see *Future Proof* on the bookshelves, you'll be able to find out the answers too.

I'm still not sure if the story is going to turn into one book, two books or a trilogy. That's a decision I won't be able to take until I see how the plot develops. But one thing I have decided is that the ending I previously thought would be *Seb and Jane save mankind* isn't going to be a *humans defeat the aliens* scenario. I've already introduced one good alien so it's reasonable to suppose there are others. As a result, I'm currently planning a *good triumphs over evil* ending where the good side are a mix of humans and aliens and the future involves both groups living in harmony.

In chapter 3, I said that the theme for a book often starts to show itself while you're working on it, and that's definitely happening with *Future Proof*. As I developed the setting for the story, I spotted signs that the themes might be freedom, democracy and courage. Although those issues are still going to be important to the story, I now think the main theme will be that we're determined by the choices we make, not our race, nationality or gender. And now I know that, it will effect the way I develop the plot.

I've still got a lot of work to do before I'll be ready to start writing. I may change my mind about many of the details if I think of better ideas, and if inspiration strikes, I'll be happy to follow wherever it leads. That's the fun of plotting: it's like a voyage of discovery, helping us puzzle out stories that are waiting to be told.

Conclusion

I hope this book has helped you discover a way of creating stories that works for you. Don't worry if your method is not exactly the same as mine. We are different people. We think differently and have different lives so it's not surprising if we work differently too.

Your book is your own. It grew in your head, and it will eventually have your name on the cover. So please remember this advice from a gifted storyteller. He's talking about retelling folktales, but his words also apply to all of us who create stories from scratch.

Some stories are ancient, creaking, old as hills beneath the sky. It makes no difference how long a story's been told for. Folklore is quite literally what you make of it. After all, and say it quiet, for here's the secret of them all: we are the folk, now. Let's tell our tales the way we want.

Matt Kimpton

Other books about plotting

I've read many books about plotting and gained something from all of them, even if it was just the knowledge that I didn't want to work that way. Here are the three that I have enjoyed most.

How to write for animation
by Jeffery Scott

Jeffrey Scott's description of how he plots a story showed me how to unleash my own creativity.

Doctor Who: The Writer's Tale. The Final Chapter
by Russell T Davies and Benjamin Cook

This amazing insight into how a writer creates stories takes the form of an email conversation between Russell T Davies and Benjamin Cook while Russell T was writing and editing scripts for *Doctor Who*. You don't have to be a *Doctor Who* fan to enjoy it, but you'll probably find it helpful to watch the episodes they are talking about. You may be as surprised as I was to see the order in which he got his ideas.

Story
by Robert McKee

This is the classic book about story structure. It talks about screenwriting, but it's equally relevant to books.

A note from the author

I love writing, and I've been a professional author for almost thirty years. In that time, I've had more than forty books published, including several several that I've published myself, and I've had five animation scripts produced for TV. I write fiction and non-fiction, and many of my books have been translated into other languages. You can find out more about me and about my books on my website.

dianakimpton.co.uk

Over the years, I've had plenty of help and encouragement from other writers. This book is my way of passing on the favour by helping you improve your skills. I hope you've enjoyed it and found it useful. If you have, please consider putting a review on Amazon or any other book-related site. I'll be delighted if you do.

Index

Made in the USA
Middletown, DE
05 May 2018